Environmental Print

IN THE

Classroom

Meaningful Connections for Learning to Read →

Jennifer Prior
Northern Arizona University
Flagstaff, Arizona, USA

Maureen R. Gerard
University of Arizona South
Sierra Vista, Arizona, USA

INTERNATIONAL
Reading Association
800 BARKSDALE ROAD, PO BOX 8139
NEWARK, DE 19714-8139, USA
www.reading.org

The International Reading Association attempts, through its publications, to provide a forum for a wide spectrum of opinions on reading. This policy permits divergent viewpoints without implying the endorsement of the Association.

Editorial Director, Books and Special Projects   Matthew W. Baker
Managing Editor   Shannon T. Fortner
Permissions Editor   Janet S. Parrack
Acquisitions and Communications Coordinator   Corinne M. Mooney
Associate Editor   Charlene M. Nichols
Administrative Assistant   Michele Jester
Assistant Permissions Editor   Tyanna L. Collins
Production Department Manager   Iona Muscella
Supervisor, Electronic Publishing   Anette Schütz
Electronic Publishing Specialist   R. Lynn Harrison
Proofreader   Elizabeth C. Hunt

Project Editor   Charlene M. Nichols

Cover Design and Illustrations   Linda Steere

Library of Congress Cataloging-in-Publication Data
Prior, Jennifer Overend, 1963–
 Environmental print in the classroom : meaningful connections for learning to read / Jennifer Prior, Maureen R. Gerard.
    p. cm.
    Includes bibliographical references and index.
    ISBN 0-87207-553-2
 1. Reading—Phonetic method. 2. Reading comprehension. 3. Reading—Language experience approach. I. Gerard, Maureen R. II. Title.
  LB1573.3.P75 2004
  372.46'5—dc22

10/19/06

CONTENTS

FOREWORD   iv

CHAPTER 1   1

Early Literacy Development and Environmental Print:
Making the Connection

CHAPTER 2   11

Play and Environmental Print in the Early Years

CHAPTER 3   25

Implementing an Environmental Print Curriculum

CHAPTER 4   76

Games and Activities for Independent Use

CHAPTER 5   101

Assessment and Evaluation: Documenting Development

CHAPTER 6   117

Getting Started: Recommendations for Teachers and Parents

APPENDIX A   120

Description of Authors' Studies

APPENDIX B   128

Survey and Survey Results

REFERENCES   130

INDEX   133

FOREWORD

Standing in the kitchen pantry, 2-year-old Annie expresses her opinions about her snack desires to her mom, who has picked up the granola bar box. Annie frowns and says, "No nola, dis tics" (Twix) reaching for the box.

Young children are remarkable creatures. Before she has the ability to use complex sentences, Annie has already begun the process of realizing that the print on the boxes conveys meaning—and a great deal of difference in taste! Annie, like all children who live in a world inundated with print, has begun to take a series of mental steps that will lead ultimately to her ability to read.

As we observe young children interacting in their environment, we clearly see that they are most likely to make these mental connections through becoming aware of environmental print. Environmental print refers to print that occurs in real-life contexts—the signs, billboards, logos, and functional print that saturate a child's world.

Although educational researchers have long known about children's awareness of environmental print, there is little evidence that classroom teachers are using environmental print as an *intentional* instructional literacy tool to help children connect letter symbols to sounds.

The authors of this book, Jennifer Prior and Maureen Gerard, are both classroom teachers and literacy researchers who have extensively studied the use of environmental print as an intentional instructional resource that transcends language, culture, and economic barriers. *Environmental Print in the Classroom: Meaningful Connections for Learning to Read* offers an extensive rationale for using environmental print as an instructional tool, and teaching suggestions for using this approach in the preschool and primary classroom. Teachers literally around the world have found this technique to be remarkably interesting to children, highly effective, and ultimately successful in helping children begin to read.

Billie J. Enz
Arizona State University
Tempe, Arizona, USA

CHAPTER 1

Early Literacy Development and Environmental Print: Making the Connection

Reading was the most valuable gift I ever received.
When I would become lonely for my mother, I would
read the labels in my grandmother's store. I would
be carried off to the faraway places on the labels.

MAYA ANGELOU
(IN AN INTERVIEW WITH OPRAH WINFREY), JULY 2003

Young children's beginning reading and writing proficiency has been receiving increased attention in the United States. The current thrust of U.S. federal funding policy is academic readiness. The hope is that greater emphasis on academics, specifically language acquisition and literacy development in preschool and the primary grades, will ensure reading success by third grade and, consequently, later academic success. The report from the National Reading Panel (National Institute of Child Health and Human Development [NICHD], 2000) has generated new early reading curriculum approaches. No Child Left Behind legislation has been translated into Early Reading First classroom practices and high-quality, research-based reading instruction. This instruction includes the following Early Reading First program goal:

To demonstrate language and literacy activities based on scientifically based reading research that support the age-appropriate development of

- Oral language (vocabulary, expressive language, listening comprehension)
- Phonological awareness (rhyming, blending, segmenting)
- Print awareness
- Alphabetic knowledge. (U.S. Department of Education, 2004)

Environmental print—the print found in a child's natural environment— serves an important part of a child's beginning literacy development. Before we discuss environmental print in detail, it is first important to look more broadly at expectations in children's reading and writing development.

What Young Children Know and Are Expected to Know About Reading and Writing

The National Association for the Education of Young Children (2001) recommends numerous ways teachers can assist children in becoming successful readers and writers. Speaking, listening, reading, and writing are not separate skills acquired independently of each other. Children learn all meaningful communication by using it purposefully in social contexts. Teachers are expected to support oral language and vocabulary development by reading and talking to children, introducing new words and concepts, and recognizing and respecting children's home language and culture. Teachers are expected to expand children's background knowledge by extending knowledge through books, field trips, and guest speakers. They are expected to promote letter recognition by focusing on the sounds of words, using word play and rhymes, and providing opportunities to write. Finally, teachers are expected to build beginning knowledge of letters in high-profile or familiar words by assisting children to recognize letters and distinguish sounds and provide connected experiences with print, pattern recognition, and decoding.

Evidence-based reading research emphasizes the importance of knowing letters and sounds as essential in reading success. According to Simmons, Gunn, Smith, and Kameenui (1994), phonemic awareness—the awareness of the sizes of sound units in phonemes, syllables, and words—is the most recognizable characteristic of proficient readers. Print awareness, or knowledge of the purposes and conventions of print, and alphabet knowledge must be interwoven with phonemic awareness for developing reading in the early years. It is important to remember that, while the identification of letters and sounds is essential for reading success, reading is, first and foremost, a meaning-making process. The ultimate goal is the comprehension of text.

Teaching writing in the early childhood classroom focuses on meaningful, interactive activities that emphasize process as well as product. This involves exposure to print in the classroom, use of environmental print as a teaching tool, careful observation by adults, and regular opportunities for independent writing. Children who are supported in their invented writing employ all their phonics knowledge in their temporary spelling efforts. This encourages communication through writing and provides many writing opportunities across the curriculum. Children should have access to a wide range of writing materials, places to write, and audiences for their writing. Writing demands that children pay attention to the details of text and integrate all their phonics knowledge into the writing effort. Writing is a process of invention through which children must construct a message letter by letter, sound by sound.

In order to learn language, children must combine perception, comprehension, memory, and attention with purpose and motivation (Block, 1993). The use of rich language environments encourages language development through interactive language activities, dramatic play, writing, and book sharing. The Early Reading First definition of a high-quality oral language and literacy-rich environment includes adults reading aloud books to children; asking children predictive and analytic questions about the book; adults' use of rich, varied vocabulary; time for children to ask and answer questions; and conversation that is directed and dialogic (U.S. Department of Education, 2004). Rich language environments also include print with which children have a personal connection posted at eye level, including the alphabet and class list; child-created artwork posted along with writing; and a variety of books of different genres and reading levels in the reading area. Whole-text literature is also recommended for instructional use. This provides children with experiences with natural language patterns in print.

Best Practices in Kindergarten Language Arts

What teaching strategies have the greatest impact on children's literacy learning in school? The following have been identified as best practices of exemplary kindergarten language arts programs (Pressley, Rankin, & Yokoi, 1996):

- a literate environment
- accessible, quality children's literature
- read-aloud experiences
- teacher–student shared reading
- numerous, regular opportunities to write
- integrated literacy instruction
- a wide range of skills taught
- home–school connections

Does best practice mean whole-group, systematic, direct instruction in reading? Are teachers merely facilitators of learning? Do children construct their own meaning and literacy through hands-on experiences? These issues become increasingly more complex when considering what constitutes effective education for children from diverse cultures and socioeconomic backgrounds. Many educators and researchers maintain that effective teaching centers on meaningful experiences for children (i.e., reading self-selected books and writing for real communication). In order to make sense of educational experiences, children need to make connections between what they already know and what they experience in school. Typically, students from economically disadvantaged families come to school with print knowledge that is not relevant to school literacy success. The disjuncture between home and school can serve to undermine a child's eagerness to learn and his or her confidence in learning ability (Entwisle, 1995).

Consequently, teaching strategies are an area of focus in relation to the education of children living in poverty. Early Reading First and Reading First guidelines demand that teachers deliver intentional, systematic, explicit instruction and conduct periodic progress monitoring to determine if children are mastering specific skills. Many experts assert that using a direct instruction model is the most effective strategy for teaching children. At the same time, there are advocates of the teacher-as-facilitator approach in which the teacher guides and instructs children in a flexible and caring manner, allowing time and space for discovery learning and inquiry-based explorations. We believe that children of all socioeconomic and cultural backgrounds learn best when they have the opportunity to be actively involved in learning experiences with the guidance and instruction of knowledgeable, informed adults who design instruction and activities that make meaningful connections for the children. A flexible curriculum that allows for adjusting approaches—as the teacher judges which is most appropriate based on the needs of the students—is the ideal for effective literacy development.

Enriching the Curriculum With Environmental Print

Many people assume children learn to read when they begin school, but most educators know that literacy development begins long before children reach school age. Children are aware of and can read print in the environment at a very young age and have a sight-word vocabulary of hundreds of words even by the age of 2 (Anderson & Markle, 1985). For example, when some children see the shape of golden arches they understand that it represents a McDonald's restaurant; therefore, they will have hamburgers for lunch. Environmental print can include product labels, logos, road signs, billboards, and store signs. Functional print, one form of environmental print, is relevant to young children because of the strong connections made to everyday life. Knowledge of functional print, such as names, directions, and signage, serves as an important communication function for young children in a literate society. Children notice logos in the community and request particular products in grocery stores by name. Marketing experts plan on young children's early reading by organizing store shelves and checkout displays so that particular products are at cart height or at small children's eye level.

Environmental print helps children to understand how written language is organized and used. Early notions about print, directionality, function, and letter sounds take shape as children realize that the print in their everyday world holds meaning and serves important purposes. Children have a natural interest in environmental print materials and often use them in their play activities. Parents and caregivers or other adults who work closely with children can build on these interests and foster print awareness by pointing out familiar print on cereal boxes, food packages, and street signs. As children become aware of and attuned to the print in the environment, their vocabulary of recognizable words grows. The young child who successfully reads environmental print internalizes the meaning-making function of reading, enjoys a sense of accomplishment, and finds a point of entry into the complex world of literacy. Environmental print is one of the first sources of reading material for young children and serves as soil for the roots of literacy.

With the U.S. focus on early literacy development, exploration in the use of environmental print makes sense. According to the Early Reading First initiative, educators are to instruct with language and reading activities developed from evidence-based reading research and provide children with cognitive learning opportunities in high-quality language and literacy-rich environments. Early Reading First guidance recommends posting environmental print because of its integral role in a high-quality, print-rich environment. Signs, logos, and other print are most certainly a part of our everyday print-rich environments and a growing body of research about the instructional use of environmental print in the classroom now can be found. Researchers Kuby, Aldridge, and Snyder (1994) have concluded that

- Children benefit from instruction with environmental print by teachers who have been coached to incorporate it into the curriculum.

- Kindergarten children benefit most from activities with print that is familiar.

- It is important to transition children from experiences with logos to the decontextualized, manuscript form of the word(s) in the logo.

- Children who bring environmental print items to school find creative ways to incorporate the print into their activities.

Reading Environmental Print: Is It Really Reading?

Studies about children's ability to recognize environmental print are found through the past three decades of reading research. Some researchers believe that when reading environmental print, children are influenced not only by graphic cues but also by social, contextual, grammatical, and language cues (Harste, Burke, & Woodward, 1982). Children respond to the graphics, color, and context in which print is embedded. Using prior experiences, reading environmental print becomes a psycholinguistic guessing game (Goodman, 1970). That is, children search for graphic cues in the squiggles and lines of print. For example, the capital letter *K* in the Kmart department store sign and in the Circle K grocery store sign are similar—red uppercase letters—yet children know the two separate logos because of the surrounding graphic and context clues that come before and after the big red *K*. Young children search for semantic cues by looking for what makes sense in the image and color context in order to read the Kmart logo. The blue background of the Kmart logo is quite different from the red circle background of the Circle K logo. Syntactic clues are internalized as grammar rules and word order emerges from reading environmental print. The fast-food restaurant name Burger King cannot be read as King Burger correctly. All the linguistic cueing systems—graphophonics, semantics, and syntax—work together powerfully in the young child's reading of environmental print.

Some researchers (Masonheimer, Drum, & Ehri, 1984) charge that no alphabet knowledge is required to recognize environmental print and cannot, therefore, be reading. There are those who say that the reading of environmental print is a precursor to conventional reading, while others claim that the absence of supporting cues leaves children unable to recognize logo words (Cloer, Aldridge, & Dean, 1981/1982). In order for a transition to occur into true reading development, these researchers maintain that children must be explicitly and systematically taught concepts about print, alphabet letter knowledge, and letter–sound relationships. Historically, explicit instruction in reading and writing has included teaching the smallest bits of language to build up to whole words. The first task of reading, therefore, would be memorizing the names and forms of letters, the letter–sound relationships, and combinations of vowels and consonants into words. Mere recognition of environmental words is not of itself assurance that children will move from context and visual cues to strictly letter–shape and letter–sound knowledge in learning to read. Children must acquire knowledge of letters, sounds, and left-to-right orientation before they can make sense of print (Masonheimer et al., 1984; Roskos, Christie, & Richgels, 2003). Studies have even shown that the children who are the most proficient readers by the third grade knew their alphabet at age 4 (Smith, 1996). Knowledge about sounds and letters is necessary before children will attend to graphic cues rather than contextual cues. Merely having exposure to environmental print materials does not naturally lead to word decoding.

In our research, we found this to be true of kindergarten children. Children do not seem to notice that logos and other environmental print contain letters, but rather see these logos as meaningful pictures. This suggests that children first must have print-specific knowledge before they will attend more specifically to the letters in environmental print. With teacher-facilitated instruction using environmental print as described in chapter 3, children began to notice the letters and sounds in familiar logos. Once they noticed these letters, they seemed to notice letters everywhere, all the time.

Our Experience With Environmental Print

Our thoughts about environmental print changed radically a few years ago during our doctoral programs when we joined a team of researchers to conduct a study of young children's print awareness and letter–sound identification. This initial study (Christie et al., 2001) focused on preschool, prekindergarten, and kindergarten children and how their print awareness and letter–sound identification increased after being exposed to environmental print used as props in play centers and in games and learning activities. We found that children at all three levels outscored the control groups in their ability to identify letters and sounds and read environmental print in varying decontextualized forms. Although we did not control for teacher interaction, we noticed that the class with the greatest gains (prekindergarten) had a teacher who used the materials with a great deal of adult–child interaction in small-group learning centers. The success of the study piqued our curiosity, and we began to wonder how environmental print could be used in kindergarten classes as an instructional tool to assist children in learning to read.

We began a search of the literature on environmental print and found that it has an interesting history, which gained positive attention in the 1980s and then lay dormant in the early to mid-1990s after a few studies refuted the benefits of environmental print and its transfer to conventional reading. Only recently has this become a topic of interest once again.

There have been many studies about children's ability to recognize environmental print (Christie, Enz, & Vukelich, 2002; Christie, Enz, Gerard, Han, & Prior, 2003a; Harste et al., 1982; Kuby & Aldridge, 1997; Prior, 2003) and debate about whether or not the recognition of environmental print transfers to the process of reading. Many researchers (Cloer et al., 1981/1982; Kuby, Aldridge, & Snyder, 1994; Ylisto, 1967) have found that after removing visual and contextual cues, children are no longer able to recognize environmental print words. The absence of supporting cues often leaves children unable to recognize them.

So what exactly is necessary for children to become aware of the individual symbols and sounds of environmental print? With adult guidance, will children attend to the letters and sounds in environmental print? Can this guided exposure to environmental print transfer to conventional reading?

Based on the results of the studies mentioned previously, we set out to test environmental print as play props, learning materials, and direct instructional activities with children in varying socioeconomic settings and with children who are second-language learners. The purpose of the first study (Prior, 2003) was threefold. The first purpose was to determine whether or not the use of environmental print games and puzzles assists in the development of letter recognition and sound identification and ability to read environmental print logos in varying degrees of decontextualized forms. These activities were performed in centers with minimal adult intervention. The second purpose was to determine whether or not letter recognition and sound identification and the ability to read environmental print words was enhanced by teacher-facilitated instruction, during which the teacher drew students' attention to the letters and the sounds they represented within the logo words. The third purpose of the study was to determine whether or not socioeconomic status played a role in the effectiveness of environmental print instructional materials in the development of print awareness, letter recognition, and sound identification. The children were pretested using an alphabet recognition test and the Environmental Print Reading Test (see chapter 5 for further information on assessments, including the Environmental Print Reading Test). During the 12-week study, the children in the control group received no instructional activities with environmental print. The children in one of the experimental groups used environmental print games and activities (see chapter 4 for game and activity lesson plans) two times a week in learning centers with no adult interaction. The children in the other experimental group received the same games and puzzles used in the same way, but also participated in two teacher-facilitated activities with environmental print (see chapter 3) each week. After posttesting with the same assessments, the results of this study revealed that kindergartners' print awareness increased with the use of environmental print materials, and the addition of teacher-facilitated instruction brought about increased print awareness with children in both high- and low-SES schools. At the lower-SES school, teacher-facilitated instruction brought about the greatest overall improvements with print awareness and sound identification.

Our second study (Christie, Enz, Gerard, Han, & Prior, 2003b) was to determine what happens to letter–symbol and sound learning when environmental print materials were infused into alphabet instruction with English language learners. The treatment group of five morning kindergarten children in the ELL program used environmental print materials including games, puzzles, books, and play props as enrichment to their typical ELL curriculum. The children in the experimental group received a minimum of two teacher-directed lessons each week using the environmental print materials. These lessons directed attention to specific letters and sounds in the environmental print words through games and activities. The control group of six afternoon kindergarten children was not exposed to the environmental print materials or activities. This group received the unmodified, typical ELL curriculum. The experimental group significantly improved in letter recognition, particularly in the recognition of lowercase letters and decontextualized words. Both studies are described in detail in Appendix A.

We believe, as our studies indicate, that with the assistance of an adult, a child is easily able to recognize the letters in environmental print. Furthermore, we believe that using these highly motivating and visually appealing materials creates a meaningful foundation for learning about the alphabetic principle. In addition, we have found that when teachers use environmental print as an instructional tool to teach letters and sounds, the print in the actual environment serves as a constant reinforcement of the reading skills the children are learning in school. We believe that as teachers implement the strategies and activities described in this book, they, too, will find that their students are intrigued, excited, and eager to learn to read. This book presents materials for teachers to re-create an environmental print curriculum.

Organization of This Book

Chapter 2, "Play and Environmental Print in the Early Years," highlights the role of play in literacy. We suggest environmental print play props, as well as environmental print play activities that we have developed, to be used to enrich play. Chapter 2 focuses on how the frequency and quality of play literacy events can be increased by including play props with text from the environment, by including literacy props that are routine in the lived experience of children, and by adapting standard games and play activities with text from the environment. Directions for creating the materials and suggestions for additional activities are given.

Chapter 3, "Implementing an Environmental Print Curriculum," focuses on the necessary scaffolding and support to use environmental print as instructional activities to teach kindergarten students the alphabetic principle. In this chapter, you will find lesson plans and game templates for a variety of teacher-facilitated activities. Lessons include objectives, materials, instructions for any necessary preparation, and step-by-step procedures for conducting the lessons with small groups of students. Many of the lessons include adaptations for use with preschool children or children who are advanced. Finally, each lesson includes an assessment to assist you in evaluating your students' progress.

To effectively use written language, young children must be able to translate the code system of written symbols into a meaningful message. The message of high-impact environmental print symbols is the first exposure young children have to this code system. Purposeful, teacher-directed instruction with the text that is high profile in the community serves as the springboard for instruction.

Chapter 4, "Games and Activities for Independent Use," presents the games, activities, and planned instruction that we have adapted and implemented with children in actual classrooms. Lessons include objectives, materials, and instructions for any necessary preparation as well as step-by-step procedures for how the games should be used by students. Many of the lessons include adaptations for use with preschool children or children who are advanced. Again, each lesson includes an assessment to assist you in evaluating your students' progress. Templates and classroom examples of the games are provided to assist you in creating these games with the environmental print that fills your community. We hope the materials presented in this chapter will inspire classroom teachers to invent their own literacy activities using environmental print.

In chapter 5, "Assessment and Evaluation: Documenting Development," we look at appropriate assessment in early literacy development. We also explain ways to use environmental print as an assessment task to measure print awareness and sight-word vocabulary. Other recordkeeping tools are suggested to help the classroom teacher to document the growth of students in a streamlined manner. The results from these assessments can be used to inform and guide instruction. This final step closes the planning–instruction–assessment loop that is critical to early literacy learning.

Chapter 6, "Getting Started: Recommendations for Teachers and Parents," includes recommendations for how teachers can implement an environmental print curriculum as well as recommendations for how parents can assist their children in learning to read using environmental print.

Appendix A describes our studies more fully and Appendix B provides the teacher survey and a sample of the survey results.

So, what role does environmental print play in reference to effective early literacy teaching strategies? This book addresses this question and provides practical and engaging uses of environmental print in the classroom, from print-enriched play environments to teacher-facilitated activities and independent games that can be made and implemented with ease.

CHAPTER 2

Play and Environmental Print in the Early Years

*Play is the purest, most spiritual activity of man....
It gives, therefore, joy, freedom, contentment, inner
and outer rest, peace with the world. It holds the
sources of all that is good...play at this time is
not trivial, it is highly serious and of deep
significance.*

FRIEDRICH WILHELM FROEBEL,
1826/1902, P. 55

The continually growing body of research in language acquisition and literacy development that we have outlined briefly in chapter 1 supports the idea that language learning is an interrelated web of skills that are acquired in a dance among cognitive, affective, and environmental factors. The impact of literacy materials in the sociodramatic play of young children demonstrates that this dance can be choreographed by knowledgeable teachers with literacy materials, play props, and environmental print. Why play? What settings influence the highest incidence of literacy play? What literacy objects encourage the longest, most complex literacy play? This chapter explores play, play props, and the literacy development that young children experience in play. It also highlights the use of environmental print materials as play props and discusses how this enhances children's literacy development.

Why Play?

To many outside observers, parents, and educators, play seems like a trivial, unproductive time in the classroom setting. This belief minimizes the importance, educative value, and developmental function of play. The early years, however, are also known as the play years because young children spend so many waking hours in play. And one of the most important domains of learning in these years is language learning. Language helps children to organize their thinking. Language is a tool for internalizing experience, and it frees children from the need to experience everything at an immediate physical, concrete level. Language bridges the gap between action and thinking; it is one of the most significant areas of development during the preschool, kindergarten, and primary years. Similarly, motor skills, social roles, vocabulary, story sequence, and peer relationships develop in play for young children. Play is the integrated space for learning across these domains. Because of decades of research in the area of play behavior, educators have a wider, more complete understanding of the invaluable role of play in the learning of young children. Play is a crucial ingredient in early literacy learning, and early childhood educators can encourage literacy development by thoughtfully orchestrating the play of young children.

Play is a complex set of behaviors that seem to defy definition and explanation. The word *play* is often juxtaposed into linguistic categories. We might think of play–work or playful–serious as categorical opposites that explain play, however incompletely. Describing the attributes and motives in play helps to characterize play more fully.

1. Children freely choose and spontaneously enter into play without adult encouragement. With the earliest stages of motor development, infants will explore what they are able to touch, vocalize, and taste.

2. Therefore, children initiate and control play, its forms, and its outcomes. Children direct what to play and how to play.

3. The motivation to play is intrinsic for young children. Play is rewarding all by itself.

4. Play emphasizes process over product and essentially has no ultimate goals. Children do not enter into play to create a specific product or outcome, though one may result from the creativity involved in play.

5. Play includes some action of the child. Even in solitary play, children mentally act on objects.

6. Play is fun! It is pleasurable for young children. It is reward enough in itself for children to continue to play without interruption for long periods of time. (Isenberg & Jalongo, 1993, pp. 15–16)

Piaget (1951/1962) drew linkages between play and cognitive development in young children in his theory of cognitive development. Piaget describes play as the action of the child on an object or on the environment. Play follows the development of the child's motor skills, physical coordination, and voice control. As the child develops thoughts and a pattern of thinking, symbolic play begins so that construction and pretend play reflect the inner ideas and thoughts of the child.

Vygotsky (1978) proposed that play creates a zone of proximal development for young children in which they are able to perform far above their typical behavior. For the young child, play allows the severing of thought from objects. The child becomes liberated from real or actual constraints in play. Internal speech, logical memory, and abstract thought evolve from the ability to disconnect thought from objects. Because play is the space where the child can think, do, and be more than he or she is, Vygotsky believed in its important educative function.

An essential feature of play, then, is its representational nature. Play includes fantasy. In pretend play, children can create and articulate the world in any way they choose. Fantasy allows young children to separate objects and their meaning or to substitute one object for another object. Representational play—make-believe play—first emerges in late toddlerhood, develops most strongly in the preschool years, and then evolves into games with rules during the primary years. Representational play, like representational thinking discussed in chapter 1, prepares children for later abstract thinking and use of literacy symbols. Blocks become a skyscraper, a desk becomes a racecar, and a ruler becomes a magic wand. The young child's representational thought processes in play allow a picture in a book to represent reality and then allow written words to represent the pictures. Make-believe and the fantasy of play are intimately linked to reading and writing in the later years.

Environmental Print in Play

Research studies that focus on environmental print in learning centers and play episodes with young children indicate that print-enriched play with adult coaching offers unique opportunities for children to associate meaning with print (Kuby & Aldridge, 1997; Neuman & Roskos, 1993; Vukelich, 1994). Exposure to environmental print items influences print awareness in young children. In these studies, interactions with a capable adult giving active assistance to children playing with literacy props increased print motivation, print awareness, and ability to read environmental print significantly (Kuby, 1994; Neuman & Roskos, 1993). Children who are aware of print and can read environmental print see themselves as readers and writers and are more proactive in seeking out print (Aldridge & Rust, 1987). Children who believe in their own success as readers and writers begin formal reading instruction more eagerly, with a deeper sense of competence, and with greater self-esteem.

How can play be enriched with environmental print? First, in planning any play center or play theme, brainstorm all the possible literacy materials that might be authentically connected to the theme beyond what is typically found in the center. For example, a home living center might have the following:

- telephone books
- cookbooks
- blank recipe cards
- blank checks
- deposit slips
- stationery

- grocery lists
- food coupons
- newspaper ads
- message boards
- calendars
- empty food containers

Next, involve children in actively stocking the center so that food containers and other forms of environmental print used by the children in their homes become part of the center play props. When children are engaged in play that comes from their cultural community, the process of becoming literate has greater meaning. Because children are personally connected to the items from home as play props, there will be a greater sense of ownership, belonging, and meaning in their learning. Children can bring in fast food boxes, napkins, cups and condiments, grocery bags, cereal boxes, canned goods, soap containers, and beverage bottles to fill the center shelves. Children can use the materials brought from home, such as newspaper ads and coupons, to write make-believe shopping lists and plan for pretend meal preparation. See Figure 1 for examples of materials and environmental print to use as play props.

Language and Play

Children typically learn about 2,500 to 8,000 words in the preschool years (Gleason, 1966). This learning occurs at the astonishing rate of about five new words per day. The length and complexity of sentences in the preschool years is equally astonishing. The typical 2-year-old child starts speaking in two-word sentences. By kindergarten, most children ask questions, make negative statements, and use expansive vocabulary. Young children learn the rules for entering and exiting a conversation, they learn to listen and respond to others, and they interpret spoken words in a few short years. Play *with* language and language *in* play accounts for much of this explosive language growth.

Play With Language. Play with language begins for the infant as sound play and manipulation of vocalizations. Infants first play with the phonological elements of language, reproducing the particular reinforced phonemes of their native language in a systematic, repetitive manner (Cazden, 1974). This form of solitary language play creates the foundation for phonemic awareness. The infant who explores vocalizations and the phonological elements of language develops a metalinguistic understanding of the sound system of language. Syntactical play follows phonological play when young children develop two-word utterances in telegraphic speech. In syntactical play, young

Figure 1. Materials and Environmental Print for Play Props

Home Living Center	Office/Writing Center
pencils, pens, markers	pencils, pens, markers, chalk
sticky notes, notepads	notepads
telephone, telephone message pads	telephone, telephone message pads
newspapers, magazines	wall calendar, desk calendar, Rolodex
cookbooks, recipe cards	typewriter, computer with keyboard
coupons, junk mail, newspaper ads	order invoices, receipt forms
empty, clean grocery containers	stationery, papers, envelopes
grocery bags , shopping lists	stamps, clipboards, chalkboards
fast-food containers (pizza boxes, etc.)	file folders, binders, paper trays
restaurant take-out menus	desk and wall signs

Fast-Food Restaurant	Grocery Store
menus, kids meal containers, bags	newspaper advertising sections
napkins, condiments, cups, plates	empty food containers
order pads, cash register, play money	cash register, play money
imitation check pads, bank cards	imitation check pads, bank cards
aprons, worker caps	wall and shelf signs
pens, pencils, markers	nutrition fliers, coupons
trays	pens, pencils, markers

Library/Bookstore	Mail Center/Post Office
books, magazines, newspapers	stationery, mailers of all sizes
check-out system, card catalog system	stamps, mailboxes, labels
shelf signs, wall signs	pens, pencils, markers
pens, pencils, markers	cancellation stamp, street maps
date stamp	postal worker cap and uniform

children flip-flop and substitute words in their strings of chatter: For example, "I'm done, done! Done bun! Dumb bun! Dumb bun!" The semantics of language play emerge when children develop telegraphic speech as well. The 2-year-old who points to a picture of a dog, purrs "meow," and dissolves into fits of giggles is playing with the semantics of language. More purposeful, complex examples of semantic play in the early years include knock-knock jokes, riddles, jump rope chants, and rhymes. After infancy, play with language requires participation with others. It is necessarily a social event and a social tool.

Language In Play. Language use in sociodramatic or pretend play helps children to plan play episodes, negotiate and carry out play roles, and talk about play events. To plan for play, children must find and use language that persuades the other children included in the play frame or pretend episode. Tone of voice, intonation, facial expressions, and nonverbal language must be considered to enter the roles of the play frame. These nuances are the semantics and pragmatics of language use that children are developing in pretend play. Children must "try on" characteristics, language, and physical carriage that match the play episode. This allows children to transform their identity and the identities of others (Fein, 1981). To talk about play events during or after play, children must suspend playing to think or communicate aloud about the pretend play from outside the play frame (Trawick-Smith, 1998). Stepping out of play frames to negotiate and discuss pretend scenarios requires that children talk about their internal thought processes. These conversations involve complex, elaborate language interaction and important metacognitive processes (Trawick-Smith, 1998.)

In order to plan, participate in, and direct play episodes, young children must have narrative competence. They must have the ability to tell and comprehend stories. Sociodramatic play demands that children construct story themes. Narrative competence requires that children know a story's character, behaviors, speech patterns, sequence of story events, and the problems to be resolved in the play frame. Acting a role in pretend play draws from considerable linguistic and literate skills in the young child. These linguistic and literate skills form the foundation of school-based literacy later in the primary years. In play, young children practice narrative talk about story settings, characters, action, motives, and problems. These elements become essential to reading comprehension (Pelligrini, 1985).

Planning for Play

Teachers can create dynamic learning environments that support play and complex literacy events. The environment children live and play in should provide plenty of material for them to talk about. Planning for play includes preparing a print-rich environment—gathering props to stimulate literacy play, allowing time to develop and enact a play narrative, and providing regular opportunities to freely explore art and literacy materials—and organizing classroom communication and classroom routines (e.g., daily agenda, menu of free-choice activities, attendance charts) so that print facilitates and supports both communication and routines.

In a print-rich classroom, children's work of all sorts decorates the classroom. The walls serve as documentation panels of what children can do. Bulletin boards are decorative and eye appealing. Daily schedules and center directions communicate the flow for the day in pictorial and print forms. Messages to children, helper charts, the daily schedule, lunch-count graphs, attendance graphs, and sign-up lists are all functional print that can be placed in a print-rich classroom for young children.

A common way to organize early childhood classrooms is to create learning centers. Centers are typically wide open, without partitions, and have labels that identify the center. Researchers have found that the arrangement of a child's physical environment has significant influence on play behaviors (Bergen, 1988; Morrow, 1989; Neill, 1982; Ratcliff, 2001). Well-defined, small play centers create spaces that seem to encourage task involvement and social interaction in play. To create small play areas that also encourage literacy development, centers should be demarcated with furniture, shelving, and hanging décor (Neuman & Roskos, 1990). Print of all sorts—student names, the alphabet, center labels, daily schedule, and material labels—should be posted at children's eye-level. Posting print in the child's range of vision makes the print truly environmental and functional for the child, rather than for the adults in the classroom. Children quickly learn to use the eye-level print as referents when exploring reading and writing on their own. Print awareness increases as children search their environment for words to copy in their writing and to match in their early reading. Children should participate in the process of placing labels around the room so that the purpose, meaning, and connection to classroom life is made explicitly for the child.

A permanent library center forms the core learning center of a print-rich classroom. This center must be a well-defined space clearly carved out by bookshelves and baskets of books (see Figure 2 for a sample room layout). Inviting "comfies," such as quilts, pillows, stuffed animals, bean bag chairs, and curtains, draw children to the library and add warmth and hominess. The library center should attract children to read; therefore, a wide range of books should be displayed with covers facing out. The center should house books of all genres and reading levels as well as multicultural books. Additional book props that can be used to enrich the library include puppets, flannel board stories to accompany favorite books, and headphones for audio books. Posters that encourage reading, book jackets from new books, checkout directions, and art should be placed on the library center walls.

A writing center is another important feature of a print-rich classroom. This center should be located next to the library, so the materials from the writing center spill into the library and books from the library "spill into" the writing process. Similar to the library, the writing center must be a well-defined area with open space for writing and shelves to hold materials. Writing materials—pens, pencils, markers, gel pens, chalk, chalkboards, whiteboards, clipboards, story paper, colored paper, blank paper, paper scraps, envelopes, stamps, and folders—should be easily accessible to children. Some teachers include old typewriters, keyboards, and computers in their classroom writing centers.

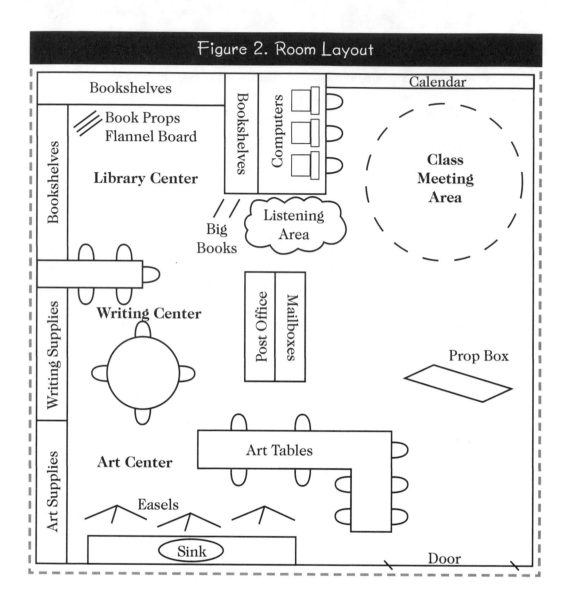

Figure 2. Room Layout

A center that is closely related to the writing center is the art center. Representation in art is so closely related to representation in language, the two centers flow into and support each other. In exploring representation with art materials, children are exploring media through the use of all senses, making random marks on paper, scribbling, and covering paper in representational images.

Additional play centers should have clearly identified, authentic themes such as library/bookstore, home living/kitchen, grocery store, doctor's office, and restaurant. Businesses and social centers of the children's community also should be used as sources for appropriate, connected theme ideas.

Few teachers have the luxury of buying whatever materials they need, whether for reading, writing, or creative expression. Free paper, including gift-wrapping and newspapers, can be obtained from local companies. Another common way to collect a variety of materials is to send home at the beginning of the school year a wish list that includes craft materials, recycled home items with environmental print, and special school supplies. Well-equipped centers need not be costly to create.

Gathering, organizing, then storing all the materials necessary for developing theme centers rich with literacy materials can become difficult to manage. One of the tools that early childhood teachers have begun developing and implementing is the play prop box. Like the dress-up box of yesteryear, the prop box holds all the nonconsumable materials of a themed play center. Unusual theme play can be reintroduced or retrieved by children at other times if all the materials can be easily accessed in a prop box.

Prop boxes can be as simple as cardboard boxes labeled with the contents or as elaborate as clear tubs with resealable lids to display the contents. Budget concerns will dictate what works best for you. Prop boxes, unlike the more typical centers outlined earlier in this chapter, can be organized around themes that are unusual or seasonal. Literacy materials and environmental print items should be packed into the prop box for easy access at a later time. Prop boxes can be made by the teacher before the start of a school year and expanded as students contribute items from home. Prop boxes can be used to pack up centers after their initial development for storage and later retrieval. Some ideas for unusual prop boxes are found in Figure 3. You also can use Figure 4 as a planning page for developing other prop box ideas.

Instruction With Environmental Print

Many research studies with environmental print show that children may recognize print in the environment, but they do not recognize the separate letters or words when out of context. As children recognize such print, teachers and caregivers can provide direct intervention. Teachers using environmental print materials in the play curriculum have the opportunity to point to individual words, call attention to individual letters, and make connections between those letters and the letters in student names, classroom functional print, and favorite book titles. This sequence of connecting signs and logos to other forms of print helps transfer to environmental print in the world outside the classroom. From environmental print, children develop an awareness of word units in context, matching spoken names and brands to written logos. Children begin to see the individual beginning letters in a variety of other signs and logos. For example, a child who has discerned the beginning letter *A* in the Arby's restaurant sign also recognizes the *A* in Apple Jacks cereal; the *A* in the

Figure 3. Theme Prop Boxes

Airport/Travel Agent	Vacation
brochures, maps, tickets	brochures, maps, tickets
airplane magazines	hotel notepads, receipts
luggage tags, luggage	luggage tags, luggage
airport-related signs	airport-related signs
travel books, magazines	sightseeing books, travel books
pens, pencils, markers	hotel pens, pencils, markers
computer keyboard	large shopping bags

Beach/Ocean	Fairy Tales
seashells, beach bag	costumes, fairy tale books
beach chairs, tanning and	posters
sun protection accessories	
umbrella, water play toys	

Veterinarian/Doctor	Farm
clipboards, record files	seeds, feed bags
costumes, prescription forms	farm implement toys
medical toys, doctor bag	clipboards, record files
computer keyboard, telephone	

Construction/Garage	Scientist/Laboratory
tools	lab coats, chemist toys
plans, drawings, automobile	clipboards, specimen displays
service brochures	magnifying glass, microscope
wood, nuts, bolts, screws	

Applebee's restaurant sign; the *A* in his favorite story character's name, Arthur; and the article *A* as it stands alone in a shared Big Book reading during circle time. The child will only be able to recognize an ending letter or a within-word letter *a* after teacher instruction, modeling, and writing experiences.

    The optimal adult interaction with children in play with environmental print does not disrupt or limit the child's play frame. Intervention should not be instructive, intentionally teaching the alphabetic principle. Rather, adults should mediate the play while still allowing children to self-direct, self-initiate, and end play frames as they wish (Johnson, Christie, & Yawkey, 1999). Mediations during play with children include the following instructional strategies.

Figure 4. Prop Box Planning Page

Implement your own play themes. Use this page to plan the items you'll need.

_____ Prop Box

Theme: _____

Dress-Up Clothes	Toy Props	Literacy Props
_____	_____	_____
_____	_____	_____
_____	_____	_____
_____	_____	_____
_____	_____	_____
_____	_____	_____
_____	_____	_____
_____	_____	_____
_____	_____	_____
_____	_____	_____
_____	_____	_____
_____	_____	_____
_____	_____	_____
_____	_____	_____
_____	_____	_____

Demonstrate

Demonstrate a particular literacy process while explaining verbally to the child what it entails. In the home living center, show the child how to write a grocery list. Then, tell the child that the cereal is almost gone, and Cheerios must be added to the grocery list. Coach the child to replicate the letters on the box: *C-h-e-e-r-i-o-s*. Point to the word and letters as they are voiced, copying the word from the play prop onto the grocery list, dictating the logo letter by letter, naming the capital *C*, and writing the list becomes the adult-mediated literacy activity.

Label

Label a particular object with print, including a letter, word, or phrase to provide a correct name for it. For example, in a play frame in the home living center, the "mom" asks the "dad" if he went to the bank on the way home from work. The "dad" wails, "Oh no! I forgot!" The adult intervenes in the play episode by pointing to a sticky notepad, telling the children it is for writing reminders, and directing the play frame by labeling the purpose of the notepad—for "dad" to write himself a reminder note. Copying from banking play props, "dad" puts the reminder note on his lunchbox for tomorrow. The adult coaches writing the reminder note as literacy activity in play.

Provide Directions and Guidance

Provide directions to expose children to a new or special literacy routine. Unlike demonstrating, providing directions keeps children actively involved in the literacy process while the adult asks questions to guide the child.

> Teacher: You want to wash the babies' clothes?
>
> Student: Yeah!
>
> Teacher: Well, what do you have to wash them?
>
> Student: Ummm, some soap.
>
> Teacher: OK, find the soap and let's see what the directions say. Do know where the directions are?
>
> Student: Here, TIDE.
>
> Teacher: T-I-D-E is for laundry. Yes, those are directions. Read to see how much this load of clothes must have. It's right here. Can you read how much it says?

The questioning strategy guides the child's "reading" of the instructions and verbally guides the literacy event with the child leading the play.

Extend an Activity

Extend an ongoing literacy activity in play by offering more information or enhancing the child's current knowledge. For example, encourage the child writing the grocery list to look for coupons that match his or her list. Matching the coupon logos to the words on the list extends the child's reading and learning from the grocery list writing scenario.

Provide Feedback

Feedback affirms the literacy events that children bring into their play. Feedback can be as simple as "Good job" to a more complex repetition of the child's words with scaffolded vocabulary use and rhetorical questioning. The following exchange in the home living center demonstrates the positive feedback that a teacher can give a student.

> Teacher: You making a list of errands you have to run?
>
> Student: Uh, huh!
>
> Teacher: Good deal! It is important to keep all that you have to do on a list.
>
> Student: Yeah, I got to go to the Walgreen's store, and to the doctor.
>
> Teacher: You have a check-up with the doctor? Which do you have to do first, go to the doctor or go to Walgreen's? Put that on your list first. Write the Walgreen's store after the doctor then you can get your medicine after your check-up!

Environmental print with the Walgreen's logo becomes an important referent for the adult to give feedback and expands the child's literacy play (Neuman & Roskos, 1993).

Children need adequate time to completely develop play frames for literacy events. Curriculum standards and administrative and parental pressures have severely limited the amount of time that teachers can set aside for free-choice, self-directed play. If play is restricted in your daily classroom schedule, we highly recommend less frequent, but much longer play and exploration times in centers. As we have shown, play is a critical part of language development for all young children. Play should be in the classrooms of preschoolers, kindergartners, and first graders. Sociodramatic play frames that are rich in complex vocabulary and full of literacy events require considerable time and negotiation for young children to plan and initiate. Research by Enz and Christie (1997) has shown that 40-minute play periods were adequate for children to fully prepare and begin dramatizations. The authors believe that 60-minute play periods are optimal in order to avoid short, simple constructive or functional play choices encouraged by brief time slots.

Environmental Print Games and Activities

Environmental print materials enrich early years play in ways other than as play props in centers. These materials make simple, inexpensive games. For example, the front panel of cereal boxes can be cut into pieces (from 2 to 15 pieces depending on the age of the children) and made into a puzzle. Adults can encourage students' awareness of letter shape and sounds by allowing students to cut out the cereal logo. Adults can provide further instruction during puzzle play by drawing students' attention to the word, letter shape, and letter name. Students also can play concentration or matching games in which they match coupons and advertisements to commercial logos. See chapter 4 for lesson plans for environmental print games and activities.

Environmental print can contribute important literacy materials to the play of young children. The essential materials are high-profile signs, billboards, and logos that young children recognize. Used by a sensitive, responsive educator, environmental print is a bridge between what the young child knows and needs to know, and translates into rich multiple literacies that the teacher can utilize to supplement a comprehensive literacy program. Chapter 3 describes how this supplemental curriculum can be designed and implemented.

Implementing an Environmental Print Curriculum

By linking the reading of words to the reading of worlds that children know best, we can spark their enthusiasm for literacy learning in school.

ORELLANA & HERNANDEZ, 2003, P. 35

Our research suggests that the adult is the key element to effectively using environmental print to teach beginning reading skills. When an adult draws attention to the letters and sounds in environmental print words, children are more likely to transfer this knowledge to decontextualized print—text without color and graphics. As previously mentioned, other researchers (Christie et al., 2003a, 2003b) have made similar findings.

The following vignette offers a glimpse into a classroom where we studied teaching and learning with environmental print. This example illustrates the teacher modeling and student transfer of alphabet knowledge to decontextualized print.

Reading instruction in this all-day kindergarten happens around a teacher table in small groups. The teacher is facilitating an activity with the students in the group, matching logos to decontextualized print. Each child has a set of logos in decontextualized forms. The teacher shows a logo and each child finds a matching word.

Miss Johnson:	How do you know that one says Macaroni & Cheese?
Matthew:	It begins with *M*.
Miss Johnson:	Do any of the others begin with the same letter?
Matthew:	Yes. McDonalds.
Miss Johnson:	Are there any other letters in that word that you know?
Matthew:	I see an *i* and a *C*.

Miss Johnson:	What letter sounds do you hear?
Matthew:	Mmm.
Miss Johnson:	Can you find an *S*?
Matthew:	I see an *s* in Skittles.
Leah:	Miss Johnson, this is so cool!

This is a common scenario that we have seen in classrooms over the past four years. Not only do we firmly believe that using a curriculum of environmental print assists children in learning beginning reading skills, but we have evidence that this kind of curriculum generates excitement and intrigue (see Appendix B for teachers' responses to our survey).

In the lessons in this chapter, familiar logos and other environmental print words are used in their graphic forms as well as in their decontextualized forms; that is, with color and graphics removed. We have found that the success of an environmental print curriculum increases when children see and make connections between these word forms.

Implementing an environmental print curriculum includes whole- and small-group instruction using environmental print logos in varying forms and independent practice with environmental print games in centers. In the typical early childhood classroom, activities with environmental print can begin during the first week of school. Many of the activities have a community-building component, focusing on familiar print related to family, culture, preferences, and the neighborhood, which allows students to get acquainted as they participate. The first few lessons featured in this chapter are ideal for introducing your students to environmental print activities because they allow the students to identify words they know and create books and collages that display their early reading knowledge. These are high-success activities that communicate that every child is able to read.

This chapter provides lesson plans and game templates for a variety of teacher-facilitated activities. When conducting any of the activities in this chapter, be sure to generate discussion about the environmental print words and ask questions that draw students' attention to the letters and sounds. For example,

How do you know that says Skittles?

What letter do you see at the beginning?

What sound does the letter *S* make?

Do you see any other letters in that logo that you recognize?

Can you find another logo that begins with the same letter?

Do those words begin with the same sound?

Adaptating the Games and Activities

The games and activities in this book are most appropriate for kindergartners, but we also have included instructions for adaptations for preschoolers or for children who are advanced. For example, pre-K children can match the same color logos or match one color logo to its corresponding black-and-white logo. Participating in these kinds of activities will assist young children in recognizing environmental print words. You can also make any game more challenging by taking away the graphics. Have the students match a logo to its beginning letter or the typed version of the word. This will encourage children to attend to the individual letters and sounds. Many of the games and activities offer alternative ways to use the templates. You can create your own games that are even more challenging. Use your imagination to provide environmental print activities that are most beneficial to the students in your class.

Determining What Your Students Know

Because environmental print is familiar to children, it is important for you to determine which words your students know and understand. You can begin by considering print in the neighborhood. What are the names of common grocery stores, convenience markets, and fast-food restaurants? What street signs are readily visible to your students? You can go to the local grocery and toy stores to see what the children are drawn to. To determine which game and product logos your students will recognize, bring some to school and ask them which ones they know. Record this information on the Environmental Print Record Sheet (see Figure 5). Also include the name of your school, nearby street names, and the names of students. It is vital that the print used for these activities be familiar to the children in order to assist them in making meaningful connections.

Students who are already proficient readers can

- find logos or words that begin with blends,
- find logos or words that have unconventional spellings,
- find logos or words that are written in cursive or variations of cursive,
- find punctuation in logos, and
- find compound words in logos.

Gathering the Necessary Materials

Obtaining the number of environmental print words needed to make the games is really quite easy, considering all the product packaging that is thrown

Figure 5. Environmental Print Record Sheet

Directions: Use this sheet to record environmental print found in your community.

Print in the Community	Familiar?	Yes	No

away. Begin to collect empty containers with common logos. Ask your friends and neighbors to "recycle" certain items by giving them to you. Collect coupons and newspaper ads of familiar products. Take digital photos of print in the environment. You can even print graphics from the Internet. For example, you may choose to use the word *STOP*, but need a picture of a stop sign. Find the picture you need on the Internet and then print it. You can even download pictures to your computer. In addition, you can send a letter to parents asking for empty containers of snacks, cereals, and other familiar items (see Figure 6 for a sample letter). We recommend that you start to fill a folder with images you commonly use. You can change the images used for your games from year to year, depending on the interests of your students.

By introducing environmental print games and activities into your existing curriculum, you will not only generate student interest but also enable your students to make strong connections to print. Students will experience success in reading environmental print as they become more familiar with individual letters and sounds. Students also will experience constant reinforcement of class lessons through their daily encounters with environmental print in the community. The following lesson plans will help you build on your students' exposure to environmental print.

Figure 6. Sample Parent Letter

Dear Parents,

We are learning about letters and sounds through environmental print words and logos. Environmental print is familiar print in your child's surroundings, such as signs, billboards, product labels, etc. These illustrated, brightly colored print items are captivating and carry strong meaning for young children.

In our class, we are spending time participating in activities that draw attention to the letters and sounds in familiar environmental print. You can help us by sending empty product containers to school with your child. See the list below for ideas.

soda bottles
cereal boxes
snack boxes
toy packaging
fast-food bags
plastic food containers

Please send to school these and other items that are labeled with print that is familiar to your child. Thank you for your help!

Sincerely,

_____

Teacher's name

LOGO BOOK

Objective

Students will create an environmental print booklet to aid in developing comprehension skills and written vocabulary.

Materials

Logo Book Template (pp. 32–33)
construction paper
stapler
supply of familiar logo cutouts
glue
pencil or marker

Preparation

1. Assemble a booklet for each child by stacking four booklet pages.
2. Cut out a front and back cover from construction paper and then staple the booklet together.
3. Cut out a supply of familiar logos.

Procedure

1. Display the logo cutouts on a table and review the names of the logos and their beginning letters.
2. Provide each child with a booklet and glue.
3. Instruct each child to select a logo to glue onto the top half of the first page of the booklet.
4. Have each child write a sentence on the bottom half of the page using the environmental print word(s), or dictate a sentence to the teacher. For example, a student might suggest "My family eats dinner at McDonald's."
5. Repeat this process for the remaining pages of the booklet. You may choose to have each child complete only one or two pages each day. If so, be sure to review the names and beginning letters in the logos.
6. Allow the students to share their logo books with one another by reading them to partners.

Assessment

Note each child's ability to identify the environmental print words and their beginning letters and sounds. Keep a record of the number of words and/or letters each child is able to recognize during the activity.

Turn the Page

LOGO BOOK TEMPLATE

Front and back covers

○

○

○

○

○

○

○

○

(continued)

Glue your logo here.

Sentence:

Glue your logo here.

Sentence:

BIG BOOK OF FUNCTIONAL PRINT

Objective

Students will identify functional print in the environment and identify the sounds made by the letters to develop the alphabetic principle and encourage phonological awareness.

Materials

bulletin board paper
stapler
glue
markers
digital camera

Preparation

1. Create a Big Book by cutting several pages from bulletin board paper and stapling them together.
2. Create a title for the book and use a marker to write it on the front cover of the book.

Procedure

1. Take your class on a walk around the school campus to look for functional print, such as bathroom, office, and exit signs. Take them outside to see the school marquee, the street sign, and other traffic signs in the area.
2. As you locate functional print, use a digital camera to take pictures of it.
3. Upon returning to the classroom, print the pictures and discuss them one by one with the class. Ask them to identify the beginning letters of the words found and the sounds these letters make.
4. Have students glue the pictures into the class book.
5. Encourage students to read and discuss the book with partners.

Adaptations

Pre-K: Ask students to identify specific words in the environment by asking the following questions: Is this the boys' bathroom or the girls' bathroom? How do you know? Do you see any letters you recognize?

Challenging: Have students label the Big Book, telling where the print items were found and the messages they communicate.

Assessment

Evaluate students' ability to identify the letters and sounds in the print they find.

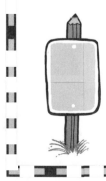

WORDS I CAN READ

Objective

Students will identify and practice reading environmental print words in order to develop phonological knowledge, fluency, and comprehension skills.

Materials

large supply of different forms of environmental print such as
    variety of familiar product containers (boxes, bags, plastic containers, cans, etc.)
    environmental print items brought from home
Words I Can Read Chart (p. 36)
Things I Like Chart (p. 37)
glue

Preparation

Display the logos, product containers, and so forth for students to see.

Procedure

1. Have students identify words they can read from the display.
2. Invite students to bring empty product containers from home to add to the display.
3. Display the environmental print items that students are able to read on a bulletin board.
4. As a follow-up activity, provide each child with a copy of either the Words I Can Read Chart or the Things I Like Chart.
5. Allow each child to select logo cutouts from the collection on display to glue onto the chart.
6. Encourage the child to read the words to you and to classmates and family members.

Adaptation

Challenging: Have students create their own booklets of environmental print words they know.

Assessment

Monitor students' abilities to read common environmental print words. Have students perform this activity several times throughout the school year. Record each child's progress with reading environmental print words.

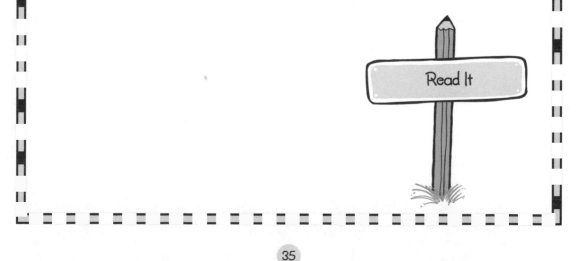

Read It

35

WORDS I CAN READ CHART
I CAN READ ALL OF THE WORDS BELOW

THINGS I LIKE CHART

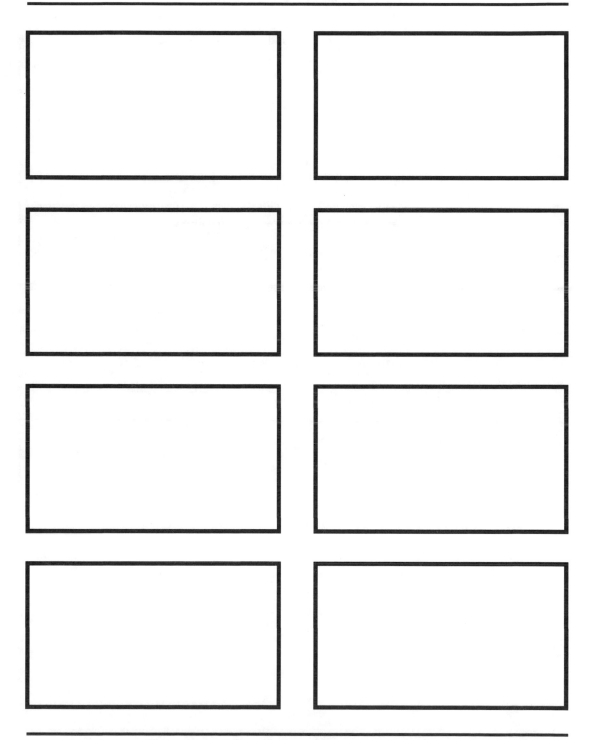

HOME CHART

Objective

Students will read environmental print logos and place the represented products in corresponding rooms in the home in order to develop comprehension skills and an understanding of the print that can be found in the environment.

Materials

Home Template (pp. 39–40)
clear tape
glue
variety of logos representing products in the home (see below)
    Kitchen: foods, beverages, etc.
    Bedroom: toys, games, clothes, etc.
    Bathroom: toothpaste, toothbrush, hair care products, mouthwash, etc.
    Living Room: videos, DVDs, etc.

Preparation

Copy the Home Template for each child.

Procedure

1. Provide an assembled Home Template for each child.
2. Explain to students that products are typically located in certain places in the home. For example, food products are typically located in the kitchen. Toothpaste and shampoo products are usually located in the bathroom. Toys are typically located in a bedroom.
3. Display a variety of logo cutouts for students. Review the names of the logos.
4. Instruct each child to glue or tape logos in the appropriate rooms on the Home Chart. For example, a Crest logo would be attached to the bathroom. A Sesame Street logo would be attached to the living room.

Adaptation

Challenging: Instruct each student to draw a floor plan of his or her own house and label the rooms. To add even more difficulty, have students glue decontextualized words on the chart.

Assessment

Assess students' ability to read logos and identify the locations the represented items would be found in in the home. Record the number of correctly placed logos.

HOME TEMPLATE

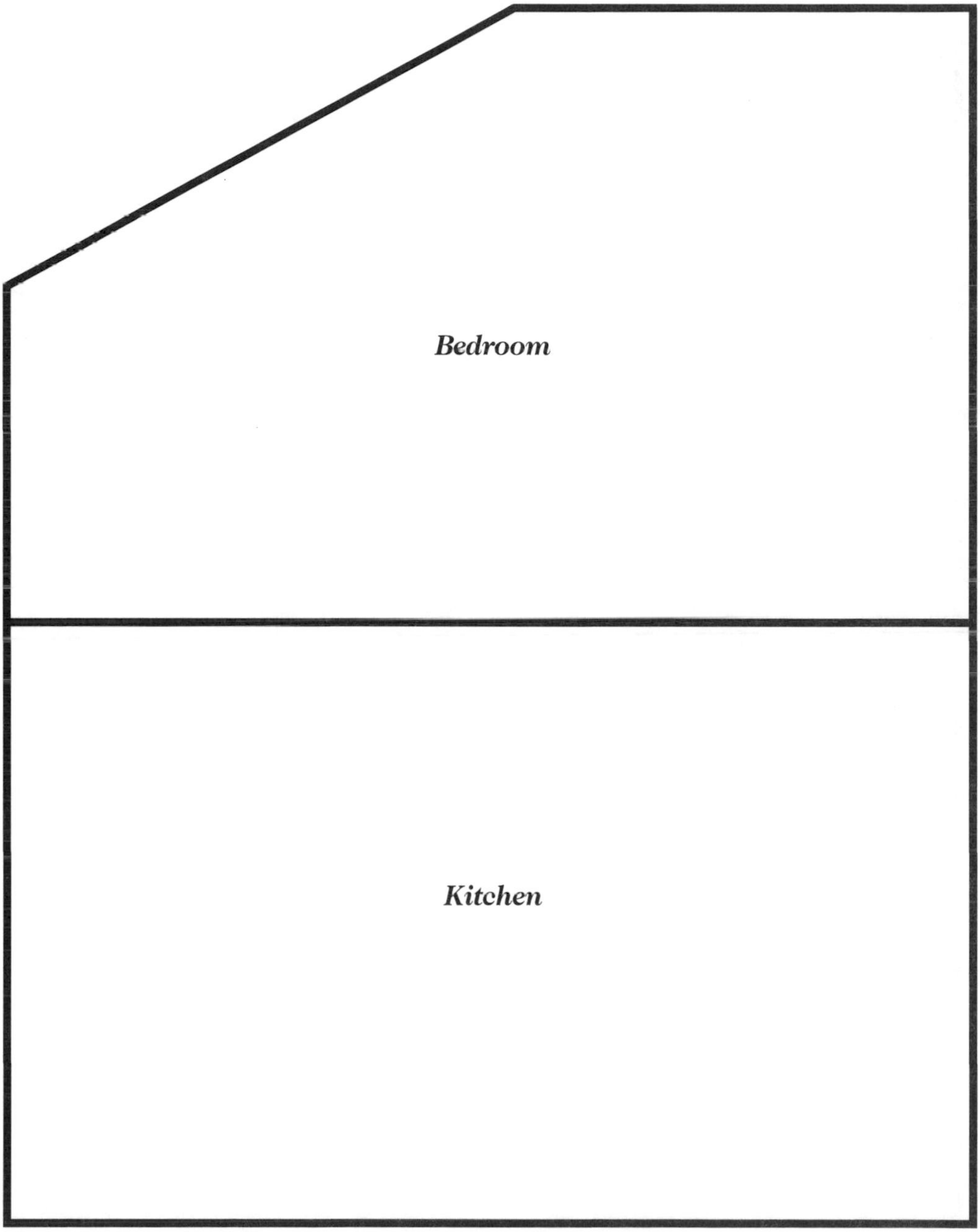

Bedroom

Kitchen

(continued)

Bathroom

Living Room

NEIGHBORHOOD MAP

Objective
Students will label a map of their neighborhood with familiar print to develop the alphabetic principle and encourage phonological awareness.

Materials
a map of a neighborhood sketched on bulletin board paper
digital photos or cutouts of street signs, the school name, nearby store signs, etc.
glue
markers

Procedure
1. Draw students' attention to the paper map. Ask them to imagine that this is a map of their neighborhood.
2. Ask questions, such as

   If this building were our school, what would the name of this street be?
   Can you find the street name on one of these cutouts?

3. Have students place photos or cutouts in appropriate locations to label the stores, roads, and buildings. Then, glue the cutouts in place.
4. Allow students to create more labels to identify other signs and buildings in their neighborhood.
5. As students label the map, ask them how they were able to identify certain words. Also, ask them to name the beginning letters they see and the sounds these letters represent.

Adaptations
Pre-K: Label the map for students and ask them to identify the words they know.

Challenging: Have students create their own drawings of their neighborhood, labeling signs and buildings.

Assessment
Evaluate students' ability to identify the letters and sounds in the print they identify.

CATEGORIZING LOGOS BY LETTER

Objective

Students will identify the sounds made by the letters in logos, and match the beginning sound to its corresponding letter on a chart in order to develop the alphabetic principle and encourage phonological awareness.

Materials

ABC Chart (pp. 43–45)

clear tape

variety of logo cutouts beginning with different letters of the alphabet

Preparation

1. Copy the ABC Chart for each student.
2. Tape the pages together using clear tape.

Procedure

1. While working with students in small groups, provide each child with an assembled ABC Chart.
2. Display an assortment of logo cutouts (facedown) beginning with different letters of the alphabet.
3. In turn, have each child select a logo cutout and read the name of the logo.
4. Each child should identify the beginning letter and place the logo on top of the corresponding letter on the ABC Chart. For example, all logos beginning with the letter *C* should be placed on the *C* space.

Adaptations

Pre-K: (1) Rather than using all letters of the alphabet to sort, select only three or four at a time to identify. (2) Have students look for logos that begin with the first letters of their names.

Challenging: (1) Have students sort logos by ending letters. (2) You might also alter the chart used and label it with digraphs and blends. (3) Without using the ABC Chart, have students place logos in alphabetical order.

Assessment

Evaluate students' ability to identify beginning letters of logos and correctly match them to letters on the ABC Chart.

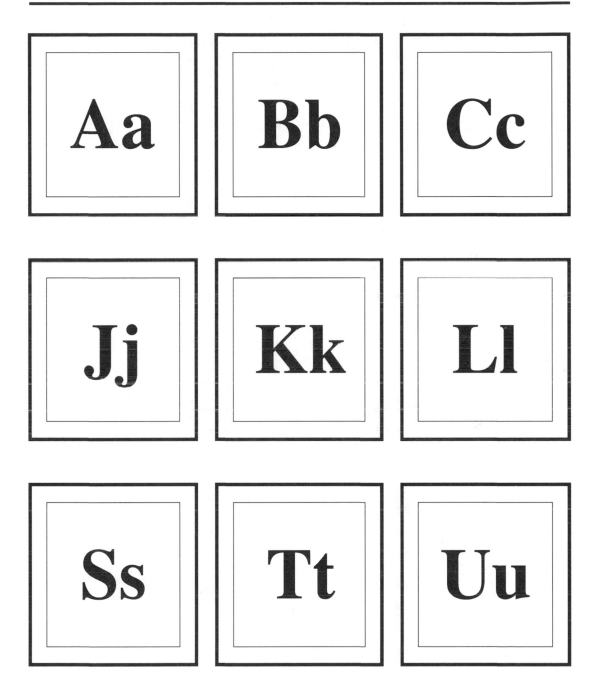

(continued)

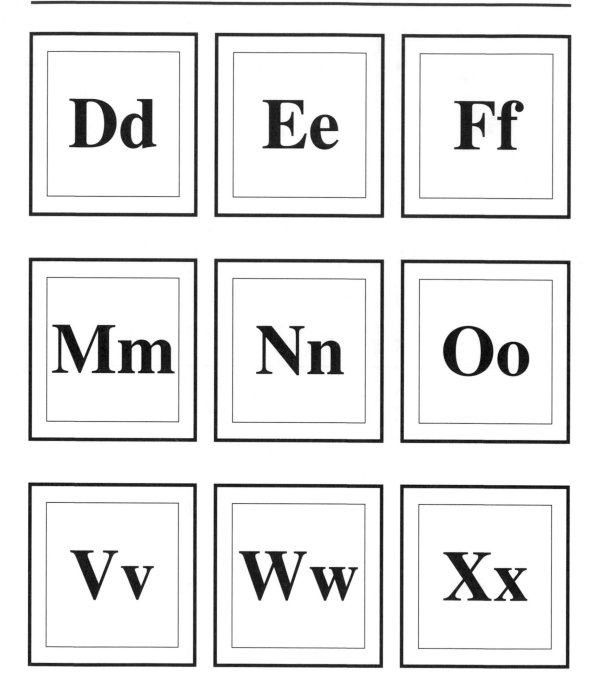

Dd	**Ee**	**Ff**
Mm	**Nn**	**Oo**
Vv	**Ww**	**Xx**

(continued)

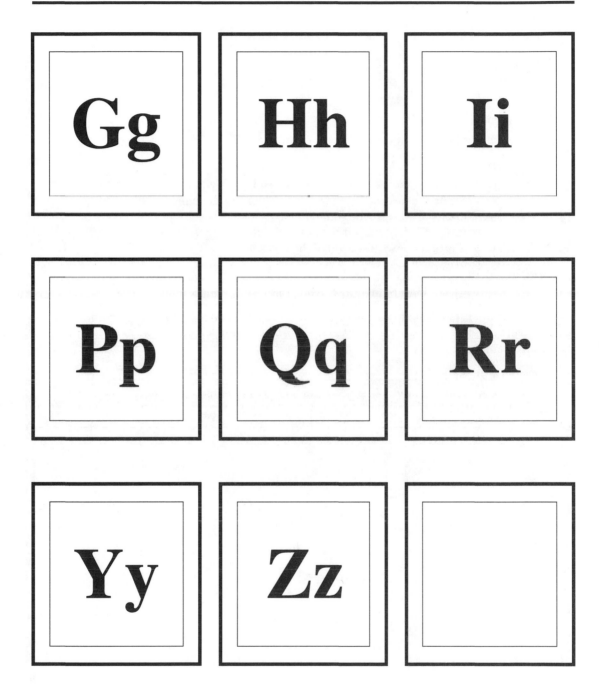

SOUNDING OUT LOGOS

Objective
Students will identify and read aloud the sounds made by the letters in logos in order to decode the words.

Materials
variety of environmental print words

Preparation
Collect familiar logo cutouts or product containers.

Procedure
1. While working with students in small groups, display a logo for all students to see.
2. Point to one letter at a time and ask students to identify the name of the letter.
3. Then, ask students to identify the sound made by each letter.
4. Assist students in blending the letter sounds together to decode the word.
5. Continue in this manner with several of the logos.

Adaptations
Pre-K: Simply ask students to identify the beginning letter and sound.

Challenging: Provide each child in the group with a different environmental print word. Ask each child to identify the sounds in the word and then decode the word for the other group members.

Assessment
Determine students' ability to identify letter sounds and blend them together to say a word. Record each word correctly blended.

S-S-Sound It Out

SORTING LOGOS

Objective
Students will read and identify appropriate categories for logos to develop comprehension skills and build vocabulary.

Materials
Category Labels (pp. 48–49)
scissors
variety of logos in different categories (foods, drinks, toys, snacks, movies, etc.)

Preparation
1. Copy and cut out the category cards.
2. Cut out logos that represent a variety of categories.

Procedure
1. Select two or more category cards to display for a small group of students.
2. Display a variety of logos for students.
3. Review the logo names with students.
4. Instruct each child, in turn, to select a logo, say its name, and place it below the correct category card.
5. Continue in this manner, allowing students to classify logos in several different categories.

Adaptations
Pre-K: Read aloud the logo name to the students and ask them to identify the category.

Challenging: Encourage critical thinking by creating a Venn diagram (see below) labeled with categories such as Food/Both/Fun. The students place logos in the appropriate sections of the diagram. For example, Taco Bell would be placed in the Food section. Lego would be placed in the Fun section. McDonald's could be placed in the Both section because most locations have food and a children's play area.

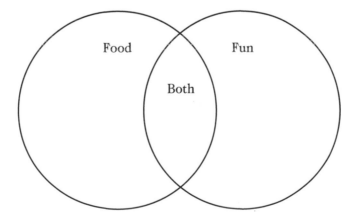

Assessment
Observe students as they sort logos by category. When a child sorts a logo into an unexpected category, probe his or her thought processes in order to understand logic.

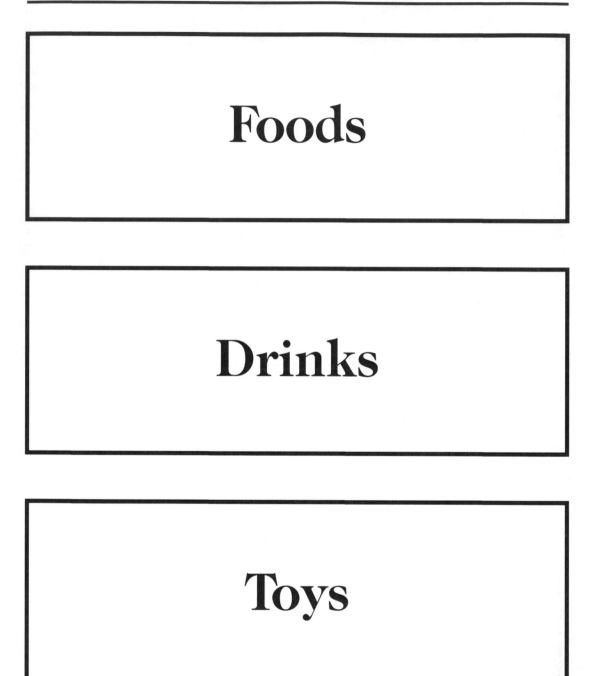

Foods

Drinks

Toys

(continued)

Snacks/Candy

Television Programs

Movies

ENVIRONMENTAL PRINT SHOW AND TELL

Objective

Students will present to the class environmental print product packaging from home in order to develop oral language skills, phonological knowledge, and comprehension skills.

Materials

copies of Sample Parent Letter (Figure 6, p. 30)
environmental print items from home

Preparation

1. Copy the Sample Parent Letter for each child.
2. Send a letter home with each student.
3. Collect environmental print items that students bring in from home.

Procedure

1. Display students' environmental print items.
2. Conduct a show-and-tell session, allowing each child to show the item he or she brought to school.
3. Encourage each child to say the name of the product and then share any other information about the item.
4. Ask students questions, such as

> How do you know the name of this item?
> What letters do you recognize?
> What sounds do these letters make?
> What letter do you see at the end of the word? What sound does that letter make?

Adaptation

Challenging: Ask students to identify logos that utilize cursive letters (e.g., Kleenex) or unusual spellings (e.g., Toys Я Us). Also, ask students to group logos that have unusual font styles.

Assessment

Evaluate and record students' ability to identify the letters and sounds in the environmental print logo as the item is shared.

CATEGORY WALLS

Objective

Students will read environmental print words displayed on a word wall to develop comprehension skills and phonological knowledge, and to build fluency.

Materials

Category Wall Labels (pp. 52–53)
colored cardstock
scissors
stapler
environmental print words and logos

Preparation

1. Copy the labels onto colored cardstock.
2. Cut out the labels and staple them to a word wall in your classroom.

Procedure

1. Display a variety of logo cutouts (related to the word wall labels) for students to read.
2. Review the names of the logos with students.
3. Allow each child to select a logo and determine its category. For example, a soda logo would go with the Things We Drink category.
4. Staple the logo below the corresponding category label.
5. Encourage students to bring logos to school to add to the word wall.

Adaptations

Pre-K: Read aloud the logo name to students and ask them to identify the category.

Challenging: (1) Have students locate their own logos to add to the categories. (2) Create index cards labeled with decontextualized words to place beside the logos.

Assessment

Determine students' ability to read the logos and identify the correct categories by having them read logos aloud as they add their words to the wall.

Use
the
Word
Wall

Things We Eat

Things We Drink

Places We Eat

(continued)

Things We Play With

Things We Watch on TV

Things We Don't Eat or Drink

LETTER COLLAGES

Objective

Students will create a word collage using environmental print words that begin with particular letters to develop the alphabetic principle, phonological knowledge, and decoding skills.

Materials

construction paper (one sheet per child)
marker
supply of environmental print words beginning with four different letters
glue

Preparation

1. Fold each sheet of construction paper into four sections.
2. Label each section with a different letter. For this lesson, we will use the letters *R, S, F,* and *K.*

Procedure

1. Provide a labeled sheet for each child.
2. Display a supply of logos beginning with the letters *R, S, F,* and *K.*
3. Review the names of the logos.
4. Instruct each child to select a logo and determine its beginning letter.
5. Then, have the child locate the section of the construction paper that is labeled with that letter.
6. Have the child glue the logo in the section.
7. Continue in this manner until the child has attached three or more logos in each section.

Adaptations

Pre-K: Have students work with only two letters at a time instead of four.

Challenging: (1) Provide decontextualized words for students to glue below letters.
(2) Have students sort words that contain different digraphs and blends.

Assessment

Observe students to determine their ability to identify beginning letters and relate them to the letters on the labeled construction paper. On a class list, record the letters each student mastered beside his or her name.

ALPHABETIC WORD WALL

Objective

Students will add environmental print words to an alphabetic word wall to develop the alphabetic principle, phonological knowledge, and decoding skills.

Materials

index cards
supply of environmental print words beginning with four different letters
glue
stapler

Preparation

Attach alphabet flash cards or die-cut letters to a section of your classroom wall at students' eye level.

Procedure

1. Display a supply of logos.
2. Review the names of the logos.
3. Instruct each child to select a logo and say its beginning letter.
4. Have the child glue the logo to an index card and indicate under which letter of the alphabet it should be placed.
5. Staple the card in place.
6. Continue in this manner until all students have had an opportunity to add logos to the word wall.
7. Throughout the year, have students add additional environmental print words they learn by writing them on index cards and stapling them below the corresponding letter of the alphabet. Words also can include high-frequency words and students' names.

Adaptations

Pre-K: (1) Allow children to use a pointer to point to words on the wall that they know. Have them read the words to the class. (2) Have students practice writing words that are posted on the wall.

Challenging: (1) Play "I Spy" by providing clues for students to use to identify particular logos. (2) Students also can perform a choral reading of words beginning with the same letter.

Assessment

Observe students to determine each child's ability to identify beginning letters and relate them to the letters on the labeled construction paper. On a class list, record the letters each student mastered beside his or her name.

DECONTEXTUALIZED READING

Objective

Students will read environmental print words in varying forms of decontextualization to encourage transfer from contextual whole-word identification to alphabetic decoding.

Materials

eight environmental print words in varying forms (see Preparation)
one index card for each child
glue
word processor and printer
scissors
three resealable plastic bags for each child

Preparation

1. Copy eight different logos in color and glue each to a different index card.
2. Copy the same eight logos in black and white and glue each to a different index card.
3. Type the name of each logo. Print and cut out each logo and glue it to a different index card.
4. Laminate all the cards for durability, if desired.
5. Place each set of logo cards in a different resealable plastic bag for storage.

Procedure

1. Provide each child in a small group with all three sets of cards.
2. Show students how to arrange each set of logo cards in a column. For example, all color logos are placed in one column. All black-and-white logo cards are placed in a second column. All typed logo cards are placed in a third column. (Cards in columns should be in random order.)
3. To play, say one of the logo names and ask each child to find it in the first column.
4. Assist students by asking them to listen for the beginning letter sound and determine the letter that represents that sound.
5. Continue in this manner asking students to locate logos in all three columns.
6. Increase the difficulty of this activity by creating sets of cards that have several different logos that all begin with the same letter, such as Macaroni & Cheese, McDonald's, and m&ms.

Adaptations

Pre-K: Display the first column of color logos and ask students to identify them. Progress to black-and-white logos, if appropriate.

Challenging: As you say the name of a logo, have students identify the word in all three columns.

Assessment

Observe students and record their ability to recognize letters in the decontextualized words.

POLLING THE CLASS

Objective

Students will read logos and place them on graphs according to category to develop phonological knowledge, build vocabulary, and develop comprehension skills.

Materials

graph templates (pp. 58–61)
logos associated with each graph (several of each logo)
cardstock
scissors
glue
adhesive

Preparation

1. Laminate the graph templates for durability.
2. Cut several cards from cardstock.
3. Make graphing markers by gluing logos and environmental print words onto cardstock cards. Example: For the graph My Favorite Cereal, make graphing markers from three popular cereal logos in your area grocery stores. Some graphing activities may require a class set of graphing markers for each of the three choices.
4. Laminate the cards for durability.
5. Place one half of the adhesive to the graph marker.
6. Place the remaining half of the adhesive to the graphing template.

Procedure

1. Direct each child to choose a favorite item from the choices offered.
2. Have students attach their markers to the adhesive piece on the graphing board.
3. Discuss the finished graph results with students. For example,

> What do you know about the cereal (restaurant, etc.) our class likes?
> Which does our class like the most?
> Which does our class like the least?
> Which two does our class like the same?
> Which is missing from our graph?

Adaptation

Challenging: (1) Allow students to select their top two favorite choices and attach them to the graph. (2) Encourage students to ask questions relating to the graph. (3) Have students reproduce the class graph onto their own graph.

Assessment

Determine students' ability to read environmental print words as they answer questions in the group discussion.

OUR FAVORITE CEREAL

#1

#2

#3

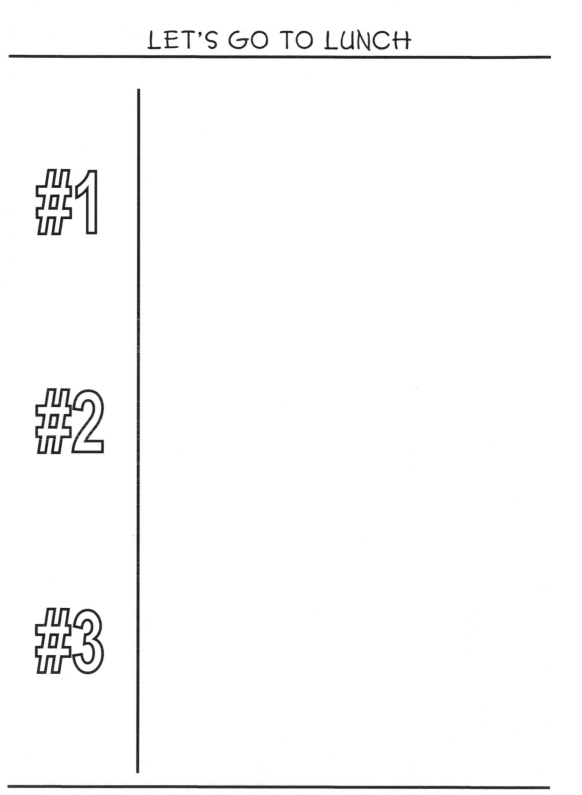

#1

#2

#3

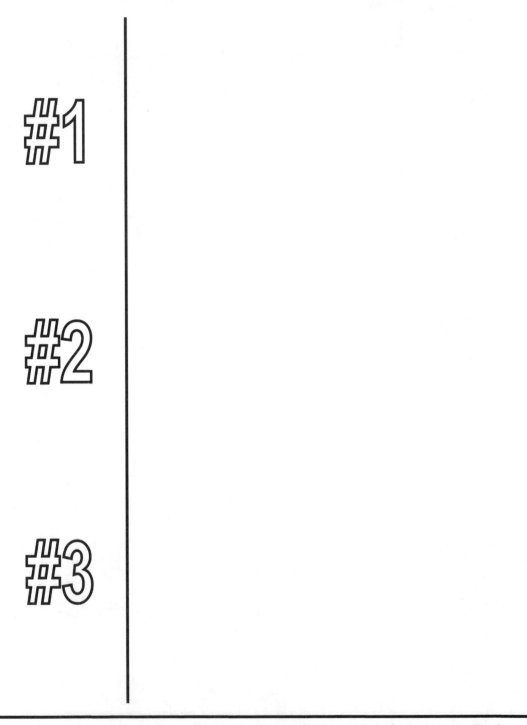

OUR FAVORITE SNACK FOODS

#1

#2

#3

LITTLE ABC BOOK

Objective

Students will develop the alphabetic principle, phonological knowledge, and decoding skills by creating an ABC book filled with environmental print, as shown.

Materials

Little ABC Book Template (pp. 64–70)
one environmental print word for each letter of the alphabet
glue
stapler

Preparation

1. Copy book templates for each student.
2. Fold each of the seven Little ABC Book pages in half widthwise and again lengthwise. (For the first page, Aa and Bb will be on the inside and the title and letter Cc will be on the outside.)
3. Each folded side of the Little ABC Book page will show an uppercase and a lowercase letter of the alphabet.

Environmental Print Suggestions

fast-food restaurants	household products
cartoon characters names	snack foods
breakfast cereals	toys
health and beauty products	movies
student names	movie posters and advertisements
street names	stores
school name	beverages
street directional signs	clothing brands
building signage	

Procedure

1. On each page of the Little ABC Book, have each child glue an environmental print word or logo with the corresponding beginning letter.
2. After ABC books are created, have students read them to a partner.

Adaptations

Pre-K: Create one ABC big book as a class. Focus on one letter page at a time.

Challenging: Have students add classmate, family, and school names as well as high-frequency words and decontextualized logo words to the books.

Assessment

As students assemble their books, ask them to name the logos, their beginning letters, and the sounds made by these beginning letters. Record the letters and sounds students can identify.

Little
ABC Book

Cc

Ee Ff

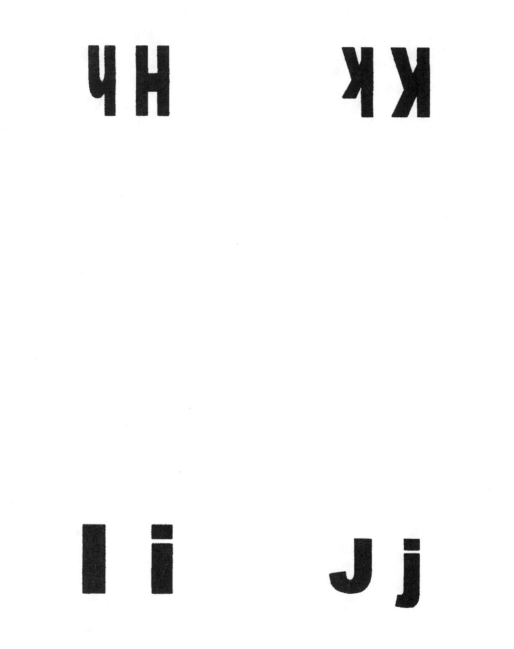

Ll   Oo

Mm   Nn

d d   s s

Q q   R r

Tt   Ww

Uu   Vv

Zz

Yy

ABC BOOK OF NAMES

Objective

Students will create an ABC book filled with classmates' first names to develop the alphabetic principle, phonological knowledge, and decoding skills.

Materials

Little ABC Book Template (pp. 64–70)
stapler
markers

Preparation

1. Copy book template for each student.
2. Fold each of the seven Little ABC Book pages in half widthwise and again lengthwise. (For the first page, Aa and Bb will be on the inside and the title and letter Cc will be on the outside.)
3. Each folded side of the Little ABC Book page will show an uppercase and a lowercase letter of the alphabet.

Procedure

1. Work with students in small groups.
2. Provide each child with an assembled ABC book.
3. Discuss with students that names of people are found in our surroundings. Ask them to think of the names of some people they know.
4. Display the names of students in the class and ask them to identify the names they recognize. Review all of the names with students.
5. On each page of the ABC book, have each child use a marker to write the names of students in class whose names begin with that letter.
6. After the books are created, have students read them to partners.

Adaptations

Pre-K: Write students' names on index cards. Create a class Big Book and have each child glue one or two name cards to the corresponding pages.

Challenging: Have students add to their books the names of their friends, family members, principal, and other teachers in the school.

Assessment

As students assemble their books, ask them to read the names they write and identify the beginning letters and sounds. Record the letters and sounds students can identify.

ENVIRONMENTAL PRINT BINGO

Objective

Students will match the colored, graphics version of logos to more decontextualized forms to encourage transfer from contextual whole-word identification to alphabetic decoding.

Materials

Bingo Template (p. 73)
index cards
glue
nine game markers per child (construction-paper squares, foam squares, game chips, etc.)

Preparation

1. Copy a Bingo Template for each child.
2. Glue a different colored environmental print logo in each space on a third of the cards. Vary the placement of the logos on the cards.
3. Glue a different black-and-white logo in each space on another third of the cards.
4. Finally, glue a different typed version of each word in the remaining space on the cards.
5. Glue copies of each logo—in each of its forms—to index cards. For example, have a card with the colored McDonald's logo, another card with a black-and-white McDonald's logo, and another card with the typed word *McDonald's*.

Procedure

1. Provide each child with a Bingo card and nine game markers.
2. Select a logo card and show it to students.
3. Instruct students to locate the logo on their Bingo cards. Tell them that the logo may not have the graphics or colors that are shown on the logo card.
4. Students who find this logo on their cards should cover it with a game marker.
5. A child who covers three spaces in a row (horizontally, diagonally, or vertically) wins that round of play.

Adaptations

Pre-K: Play small-group Bingo with only one Bingo card. A logo is selected and students identify the name. As a group, students find the logo on the card and cover it with a game marker.

Challenging: (1) Students may also play until they get "black out," where all spaces of the card are covered by a marker. (2) Provide each child with more than one Bingo card with differing levels of decontextualization to play at the same time.

Assessment

Copy the Bingo cards to create assessment sheets. As a child reads aloud a logo name, write that child's name beside the word on your copy of the Bingo card, indicating that he or she is able to read that word.

BINGO TEMPLATE

FOOD AND FUN

Objective

Students will read environmental print words and sort them into categories to develop phonological awareness, build vocabulary, and develop comprehension skills.

Materials

Food and Fun Template (p. 75)
supply of logos that represent food and fun (see list below)
scissors
glue

Preparation

1. Copy the Food and Fun Template for each student.
2. Gather a supply of logos that represent food and fun and cut them out.
3. Spread out the logos on a table.

Procedure

1. Explain to students that they will read logos and decide if they represent food or fun. For example, show students a Pokémon logo. Ask them to say the name of the logo. Then ask, "Is Pokémon food or something that is fun?" Explain that this logo would be glued below the label "Fun."
2. Have students select logos and then determine the correct category.
3. Have each child glue the logo below the corresponding label.

Food Logos

fast-food restaurants, pizza parlors, cereal, desserts, chips, etc.

Fun Logos

toys, television program logos, etc.

Adaptations

Pre-K: Reduce the number of logos students are required to sort.

Challenging: (1) Increase the difficulty by creating a chart with three or four categories. (2) Have students glue on decontextualized words.

Assessment

Listen to students as they read logo names. Look at students' Food and Fun charts to make sure logos are glued below the correct categories.

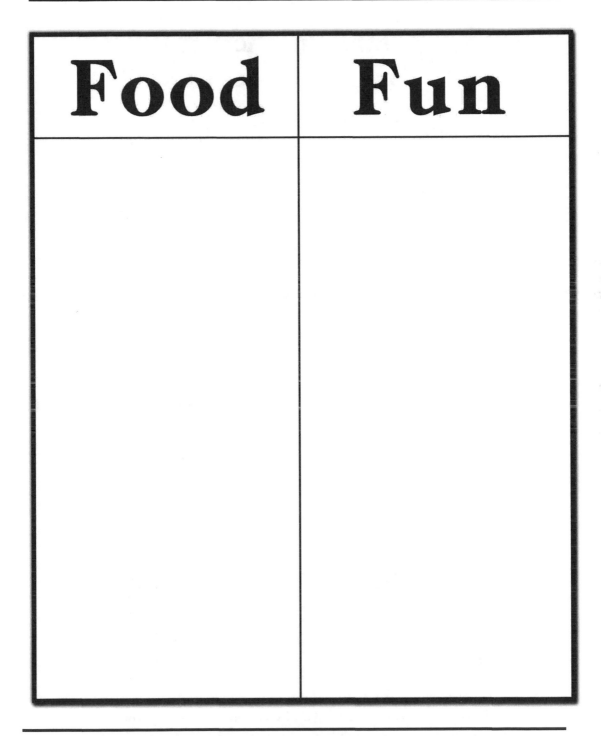

Food	Fun

CHAPTER 4

Games and Activities for Independent Use

Alphabet knowledge is driven by the child's awareness of print.... "Play-doh starts with P—/p/—/p/—P."

PRIOR, 2003, P. 147

It is literacy center time in this all-day kindergarten classroom. A buzz of activity and chatter fills the classroom. A group of children are busy sorting, cutting, and pasting. Two boys begin putting together a puzzle made out of a cut-up cereal box:

Michael: We are smart of [able to read] the [words] Cocoa Puffs.

David: Look, this is Trix.

Two girls are making the sounds of the letters in the cereal book. One girl sounds out *Corn Flakes*. All the children stay busy, playing one game after another. The children realize that one of the *S* logos is missing. They all stop what they are doing to search for the missing logo.

Michael: Is it *Sesame Street*?

David: Is it *Skittles*?

Michael: No, *Skittles* is right here.

Children are often seen interacting with one another and discussing the letters and sounds in product names, not just discussing the products. Based on our studies, children's independent use of environmental print games in literacy centers and independent centers is motivational and an effective way to review their newly learned skills. Remember, however, that in order for these materials to be effective in helping children transition to conventional reading, there must first be adult involvement to draw students' attention to the letters and sounds in the environmental print. We recommend that teachers begin by using the whole-class and small-group activities featured in chapter 3, and once students have gained proficiency with the activities then introduce the independent games and activities in this chapter.

This chapter includes the many environmental print games and activities we developed for our research studies. The games and activities are presented in a logical sequence, but they can be used in any order that seems appropriate for the needs of your students. You will find instructions for playing the games as well as game templates and directions for assembly. In addition to these materials, you can use the Independent Games and Activities Assessment chart (see Figure 7) to record notes about your students' interactions with the materials. This information can be used for future instructional planning.

Our experiences have shown us how exciting and valuable work with these activities is—for students and teachers. Through students' involvement in the games and activities that follow, they will build a solid foundation for future reading experiences.

Figure 7. Independent Games and Activities Assessment

Directions: Use this sheet to record your students' responses to their independent use of environmental print games and activities.

Game/ Activity	Student's Level	Interest Variations	Additional Comments

LOGO CONCENTRATION

Objective
Students will identify and match environmental print logos to develop phonological awareness, build vocabulary, and develop comprehension skills.

Materials
Logo Concentration Game Cards (p. 80)
scissors
four logos
two copies of each logo
glue
rubber band or envelope

Preparation
1. Copy and cut out the game cards.
2. Make two copies of the four logos.
3. Glue a logo onto each card as shown. Laminate the cards for durability.
4. Bundle each set of game cards using a rubber band or by placing the cards in an envelope.

Procedure
1. Have students place their cards facedown.
2. Each child should turn over two cards.
3. If the cards match, the child makes a pair. If the cards do not match, the cards are turned facedown and play continues.

Adaptations
Pre-K: Have students match color and black-and-white logos.

Challenging: Have students match color logos with typed words. Have students match logos with beginning letters.

Assessment
Observe students as they play the game to determine their ability to match logos.

LOGO CONCENTRATION GAME CARDS

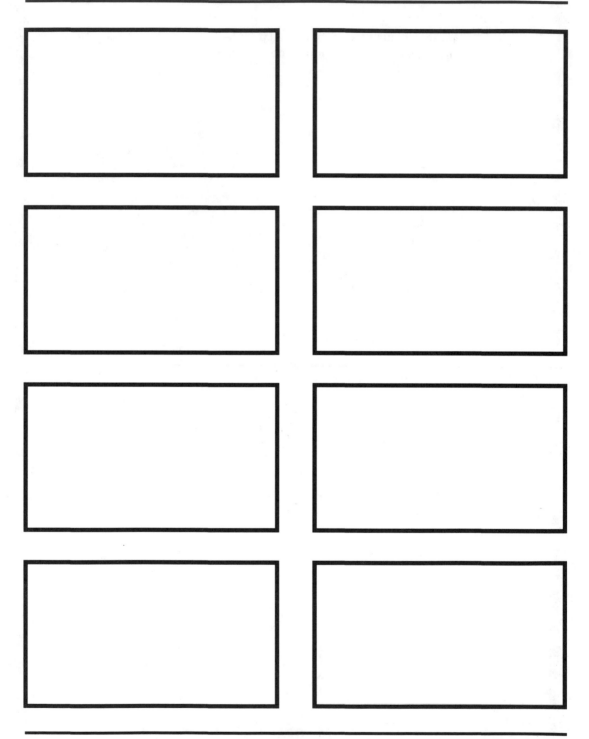

TWO-PIECE PUZZLES

Objective
Students will match environmental print logos to the corresponding decontextualized words to encourage transfer from contextual whole-word identification to alphabetic decoding.

Materials
Two-Piece Puzzle Templates (pp. 82–83)
cardstock
eight logos
typed form of each logo word
scissors
glue

Preparation
1. Copy the puzzles onto cardstock.
2. Glue a logo on the lower half of each puzzle and a typed word on the upper half of each puzzle.
3. Laminate the puzzles for durability and cut them apart.

Procedure
Have students assemble puzzles by matching each logo to the correct typed word.

Adaptations
Pre-K: Have students match the completed puzzle version of the logo to the original logo or color logo to black-and-white logo.

Challenging: Glue a logo to the lower half and the corresponding beginning letter to the upper half of each puzzle. (You may want to use copies of the ABC cards featured in the Letter Sorting game [see p. 91].)

Assessment
Determine students' ability to match logos to typed words. Ask each child to explain how he or she was able to determine each match.

It's a Match

TWO-PIECE PUZZLE TEMPLATE

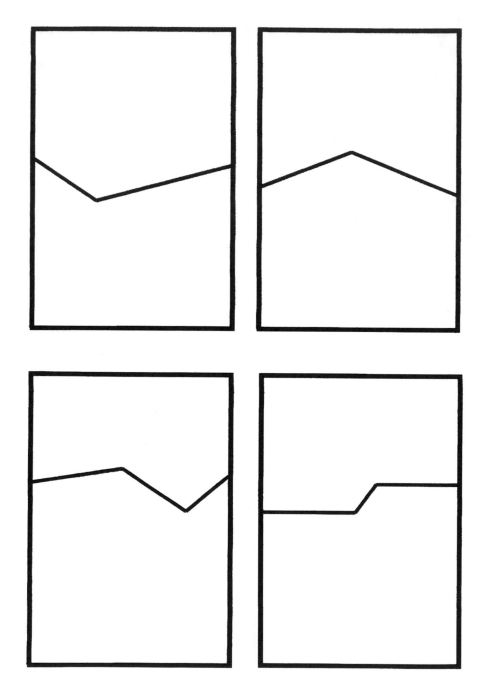

(continued)

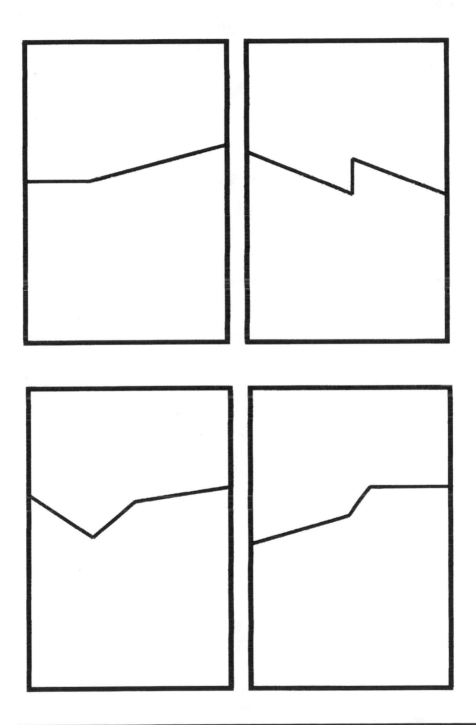

FOOD, FUN, AND CANDY BOOKS

Objective
Students will read environmental print words to develop phonological awareness, build vocabulary, and develop comprehension skills.

Materials
file folders
marker
food logos, toy or television and movie related logos, candy logos
glue

Preparation
1. Label the front of each file folder with a different title, such as *Food Book* or *Candy Book*.
2. Glue several logos inside each file folder. Laminate the folders for durability.

Procedure
1. Place the "books" in your classroom library.
2. Allow students to select the books to read independently or with partners during free time.

Adaptation
Challenging: Prepare the books by gluing logos on one side of the folder and matching decontextualized words on the other side. Instruct students to match logos and decontextualized words by connecting them with a line drawn with a wipe-off marker.

Assessment
Observe students as they read the books to determine their ability to read the logos.

Reading
Is
Fun

CEREAL BOOK

Objective
Students will read the names of different breakfast cereals to develop phonological awareness, build vocabulary, and develop comprehension skills.

Materials
front panels of several cereal boxes
hole puncher
cardstock
scissors
small metal ring

Preparation
1. Cut the front panel off of several cereal boxes.
2. Use a hole puncher to punch a hole in the upper left corner of each cereal box panel.
3. Stack the panels.
4. Cut a book cover from cardstock and punch a hole in the upper left corner.
5. Place the cover on top of the stack and bind the book together with a small metal ring.

Procedure
1. Place the cereal book in your classroom library.
2. Allow students to read the book independently or with partners during free time.

Assessment
Observe students read the book to determine their ability to read the cereal names.

LOGO OUT

Objective

Students will identify the text associated with logos to develop phonological awareness, build vocabulary, and develop comprehension skills.

Materials

various product graphics (cereal box panels, soda can cartons, pizza box logos, DVD covers, etc.)
scanner
computer
photo enhancement software
adhesive

Preparation

1. Enlarge color graphics of products and scan them onto your computer.
2. Use a photo enhancement program to erase the logo words, leaving only the graphics.
3. Make another copy of only the logo words.
4. Cut the logo word text so that it fits in the space where the text was erased on the graphic.
5. Laminate the graphics and the words and place a piece of adhesive on the back of the text cutout and on the front of the graphic.
6. Repeat this process for several different logos.

Procedure

Have each child attach the logo word(s) to the correct graphic.

Adaptations

Pre-K: Have students orally identify the words that belong in each blank space.

Challenging: Mix up logo placement and have students rearrange the logos.

Assessment

Observe students to determine whether they are able to match each text cutout to the correct graphic.

GO FISH

Objective

Students will read environmental print words and request words to make matched pairs to develop phonological awareness, build vocabulary, and develop comprehension skills.

Materials

32 game cards (p. 80)
cardstock
two each of 16 logos
glue
scissors

Preparation

1. Copy the cards onto cardstock and cut them out.
2. Copy two each of four logos.
3. Glue a logo on each card. Laminate the cards for durability.

Procedure

1. Two players each receive eight cards.
2. The remaining cards are placed in the center for a draw pile.
3. Player 1 asks Player 2 for a game card logo or environmental print word.
4. If Player 2 holds the card, it is given to Player 1.
5. If Player 2 does not hold the card, he or she says "Go Fish."
6. Player 1 draws from the draw pile.
7. When a player holds two matching logos, he or she sets the cards aside. Play continues until all words have been matched.

Adaptations

Pre-K: Concentration game cards may be added to a word wall for phonological awareness development.

Challenging: Concentration game cards may be used to quiz for spelling drill and practice.

Assessment

Observe as students play the game to determine their ability to read environmental print words and match them to make pairs.

FLIP BOOK

Objective

Students will match logos with their beginning letters to develop the alphabetic principle, phonological awareness, and decoding skills.

Materials

Flip Book Template (pp. 89–90)
cardstock
scissors
marker
hole puncher
four small metal rings
four different logos (each beginning with a different letter)
four small construction-paper squares

Preparation

1. Cut out the front and back covers from construction paper.
2. Use a marker to write a title on the front cover.
3. Cut out the book pages and then cut each one in half on the bold line.
4. Use a hole puncher to punch holes where indicated.
5. Assemble the book using small metal rings. There should be four half pages on the top and four on the bottom (between the covers).
6. Make a copy of four different logos. Glue a different logo to each top page.
7. Write a corresponding alphabet letter on each construction-paper square and glue each one (in random order) to a different lower half page, as shown.

Procedure

Have students look at a logo on a top page and then flip the lower pages to find the matching beginning letter.

Adaptations

Pre-K: Make the Flip Book with the same logos on the top and bottom pages to match or have students match color to black-and-white logos.

Challenging: In place of beginning letters, attach the typed form of the logo.

Assessment

Observe as students search for letters that match beginning letters of logos. Listen to determine whether or not students say the sounds or logo names aloud.

FLIP BOOK TEMPLATE

Front and back covers

(continued)

Glue your logo here.

Glue your logo here.

LETTER SORTING

Objective

Students will sort logos by their beginning letters to develop the alphabetic principle, phonological awareness, and decoding skills.

Materials

Letter Sorting Cards (pp. 92–94)
one file folder
glue
four library book pockets (or envelopes)
marker
adhesive
scissors
logos beginning with each of the three featured letters (five of each)

Preparation

1. Glue one library book pocket on the left side of the open file folder.
2. Use a marker to label the pocket "Logos."
3. Glue three pockets on the right side.
4. Attach a piece of adhesive to the front of each pocket.
5. Copy and laminate the Letter Sorting cards.
6. Cut the cards apart and place a piece of adhesive on the back of each.
7. Select three letter cards and attach them to the pockets.
8. Fill the Logos pocket with logo cutouts beginning with the three featured letters.

Procedure

1. Have each child select a logo from the Logos pocket.
2. Each child should read the logo and place it in the matching letter pocket.
3. Continue playing until all logos have been placed in the correct pockets.

Adaptations

Pre-K: Ask students to sort logos that match any letter in the logo to the letter on the envelope.

Challenging: In place of beginning letters, attach the typed form of the logo or have students sort logos by ending letters.

Assessment

As students play the game, listen as they pronounce the words. Observe to be sure that they place the word cutouts in the correct pockets.

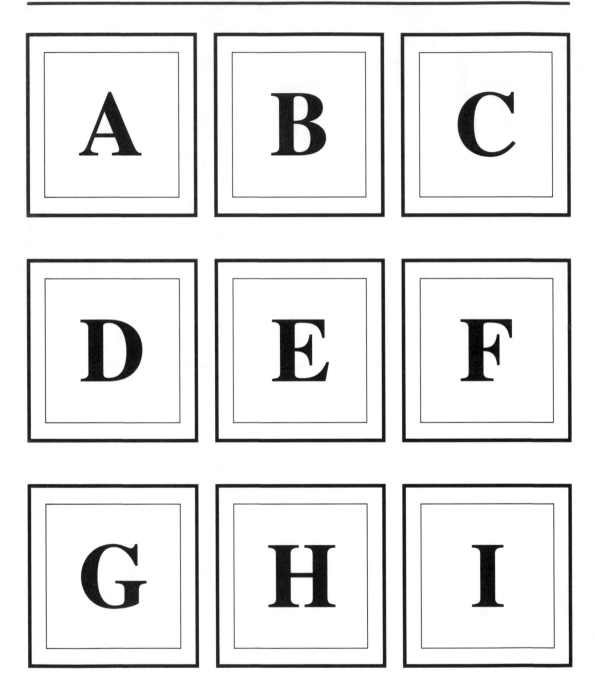

(continued)

Environmental Print in the Classroom: Meaningful Connections for Learning to Read
by Jennifer Prior and Maureen R. Gerard © 2004. Newark, DE: International Reading Association.
May be copied for classroom use.

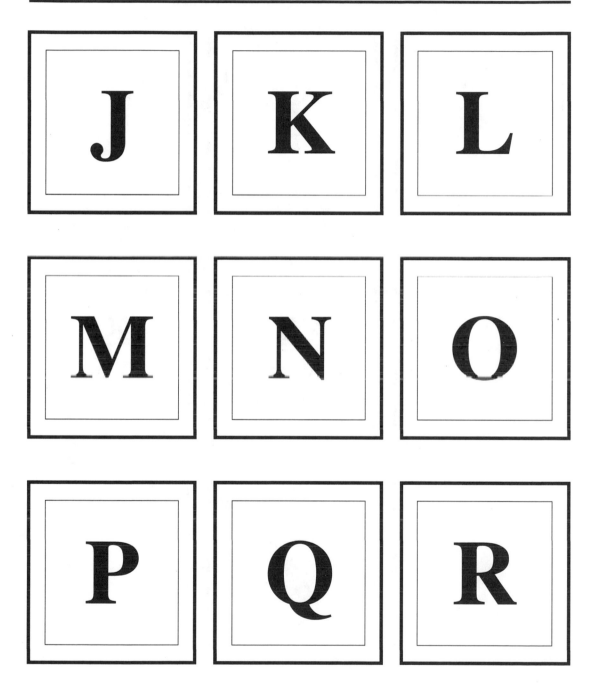

(continued)

LETTER SORTING CARDS (cont.)

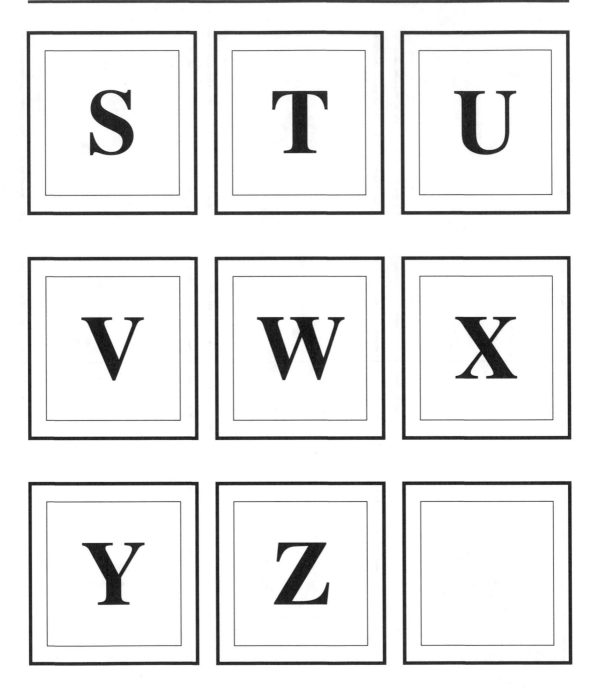

SPINNER GAME

Objective

Students will identify the beginning letters of several logos to develop the alphabetic principle, phonological awareness, and decoding skills.

Materials

Spinner Game Board (pp. 96–97)
cardstock
clear tape
eight logos (adjust size to fit spaces on spinner)
scissors
glue
brass fastener
large paperclip

Preparation

1. Copy the game board halves on cardstock.
2. Tape the two halves of the game board together.
3. Cut out eight small logos (adjust size as needed using a copy machine) and glue each one to a different section of the spinner circle.
4. Press a brass fastener through the center of the spinner. Spread the fastener tails to secure them.
5. Attach a paperclip to the fastener. Adjust the tails of the fastener to make the paperclip spin freely.
6. Label each square on the game board with a different letter. (Several squares will have the same letters.) Be sure the letters are the same beginning letters featured on the spinner logos.

Procedure

1. Have each child place a game marker on START.
2. Player 1 spins the spinner and reads the word the paperclip points to.
3. Player 1 finds the first square in the letter trail that contains the logo's beginning letter and moves his or her game marker to that square.
4. Player 2 takes a turn in the same manner.
5. Play continues until one player reaches FINISH.

Adaptations

Pre-K: Label the squares on the game board with logos that match those on the spinner. The student moves his or her game piece to the first square that has the same logo indicated on the spinner.

Challenging: Label the squares on the game board with the ending letters of the logos on the spinner. Students move their game pieces to indicate the logos' ending letters.

Assessment

Observe as students play the game to determine their ability to read logos and identify beginning letters.

SPINNER GAME BOARD

START

FINISH

(continued)

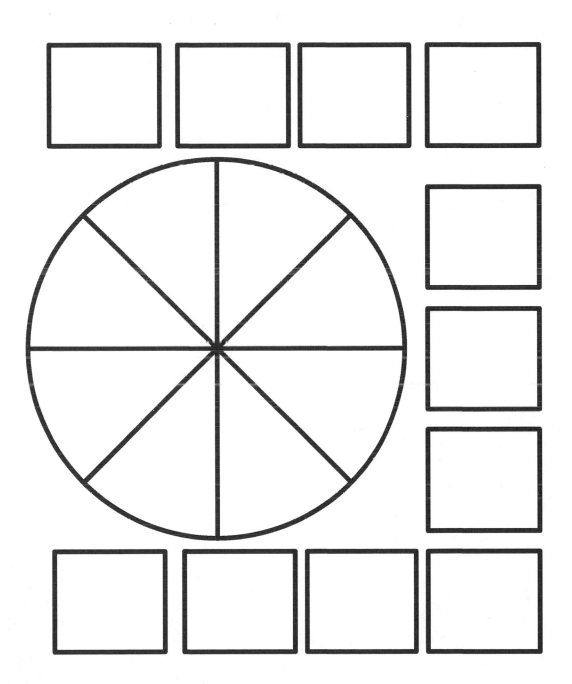

TWO-LETTER FOLDER

Objective
Students will sort logos by beginning letter to develop the alphabetic principle, phonological awareness, and decoding skills.

Materials
file folder
laminated logos beginning with two different letters (such as *B* and *C*)
scissors
adhesive

Preparation
1. Write a different letter on each side of a file folder. (You also can use the Letter Sorting cards on pp. 92–94.)
2. Cut out and laminate several logos beginning with the featured letters.
3. Place one half of a piece of adhesive on the back of each logo. Place the other half of the adhesive on the folder below the corresponding letter.

Procedure
1. Have a child select and read a logo.
2. The child determines the beginning letter of the logo.
3. The child attaches the logo to the correct side of the folder.
4. Play continues in this manner until all logos have been attached to the correct halves of the folder.

Adaptation
Challenging: Instruct students to sort the logos by ending letters.

Assessment
Observe to determine whether or not students are able to sort the logos according to their beginning letters.

Focus
on
Two

MATCHING PRODUCT AND LOGO

Objective

Students will identify and read a logo and match it to a picture of a corresponding object to develop comprehension skills.

Materials

laminated logos and pictures of products represented by the logos
laminated file folder
wipe-off marker

Preparation

Cut out and laminate logos and the pictures they represent, such as a McDonald's logo and a picture of a hamburger.

Procedure

Have a child match each logo to a picture of the item by drawing a line with a wipe-off marker to connect them.

Examples

toothpaste logo/picture of a toothy smile
toy logo/picture of the toy
cereal logo/picture of a bowl of cereal

Assessment

Observe to determine students' ability to match logos with product pictures.

Picture
It

BIG PUZZLES

Objective

Students will assemble puzzles of familiar product graphics to develop phonological awareness, build vocabulary, and develop comprehension skills.

Materials

soda can carton, pizza box, etc.
cardstock
scissors
manila envelope

Preparation

1. Select a product graphic and duplicate two copies of it onto cardstock.
2. Cut one of the cardstock sheets into approximately 8 to 12 pieces.
3. Store puzzle pieces and the original graphic in a manila envelope.

Procedure

Have students work in pairs to assemble the puzzle, using the original graphic as a guide.

Assessment

Observe as students assemble the puzzle. Listen for discussion of the puzzle graphic. Make note of students' comments about the letters in the puzzle.

Put It Together

CHAPTER 5

Assessment and Evaluation: Documenting Development

We realized that the best way of finding out what mattered to the children was to simply listen to them and watch them, rather than to quiz them with our preformulated questions.

ORELLANA AND HERNANDEZ, 2003, P. 32

Now that you have the materials necessary to begin a curriculum of environmental print, you will need a method of assessing children's print awareness and knowledge of letters and sounds. Assessments document progress in early literacy development. Because children in the early years have such differing experiences with literacy, any single method of assessment is inadequate by itself. Formal assessments are inappropriate for young children because these assessments tend to narrow the early childhood curriculum and decrease the quality of early childhood programs (International Reading Association, 1999). Measurement-driven curriculum in the early years encourages homogenous grouping of young children, minimalist academic objectives, behavioral compliance, and one-dimensional, teacher-directed instruction. Assessment formats that place observing the child and analyzing student learning within the classroom, moment-to-moment, form the core of an early literacy curriculum. The most appropriate assessment formats observe, record, and document what children do, how they do it, and how they think while they do it.

Specifically, assessment of literacy development must be based on the assumption that most children are continuously learning about print within the environment. Children who are often read stories have developed understanding of print. Children who hear many stories in an oral tradition, rather than in a lapreading manner, develop a deep understanding of story structure and know that story entertains, accounts for history and folk wisdom, and teaches life lessons. All children can enjoy and be engaged by literacy materials despite diverse experiences, and all children—no matter what their prior experiences with text—will have experiences with environmental print. Therefore, the Environmental Print Reading Test is an appropriate performance assessment. Real, high-profile items, with the logo intact, capture interest, increase initial reading success with young children because of their visual power, and begin a core early sight-word vocabulary. The Environmental Print Reading Test is short, based on 10 real items, and yields high-quality data about the child's prior experiences, print awareness, letter recognition, and levels of emergent literacy.

Creating an Environmental Print Reading Test

Environmental print assessments determine the level of logographic reading and environmental print children can recognize, the extent of their print awareness, and the strength of transfer knowledge to decontextualized manuscript text. Loosely following the design of Cloer, Aldridge, and Dean (1981/1982), this Environmental Print Reading Test assesses four developmental levels of environmental print recognition. To create your own Environmental Print Reading Test, carefully select 10 items that appear in your local area. Survey grocery stores, fast-food restaurants, billboards, street names, and road signs immediately surrounding your school. Use the empty containers and print items that children bring from home to contribute to learning activities in the classroom. These 10 real items become Level 1 of the

Figure 8. Environmental Print Assessment: Level 1

assessment—logo graphic reading of the real item (see Figure 8). Only 10 items are recommended to avoid possible frustration with a lengthy assessment. However, many more than 10 logos will be recognizable by your students.

To create Level 2 of the test, the logos of the 10 items in Level 1 must be abstracted from the item context. Level 2 is a two-dimensional representation of the three-dimensional representation of Level 1. The logo can be cut off a product container, cut out from a newspaper ad, or downloaded from the Internet by copying and pasting the logo graphic. Glue the logo onto an index card. The color, background characteristics, and other visual clues remain with the logo, yet are reproduced onto cards with the real object missing (see Figure 9).

Level 3 of the test is further abstracted from the three-dimensional, real item of Level 1 by copying the logo in black and white and removing all color cues. The 10 matching black-and-white logos also must be glued down, preferably on a set of differently colored cards. All background details are missing so that only the logo in its peculiar font style shows on the card (see Figure 10).

The final level of the test is Level 4. These cards are the typed, manuscript form of the logo in a consistent font style (see Figure 11). If letters in the logo appear in capitals, this should transfer to the printed card. You can use the Environmental Print Reading Test Score Sheet (see Figure 12) with your specific test items.

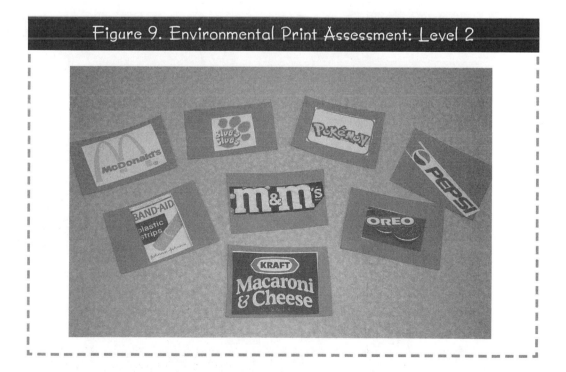

Figure 9. Environmental Print Assessment: Level 2

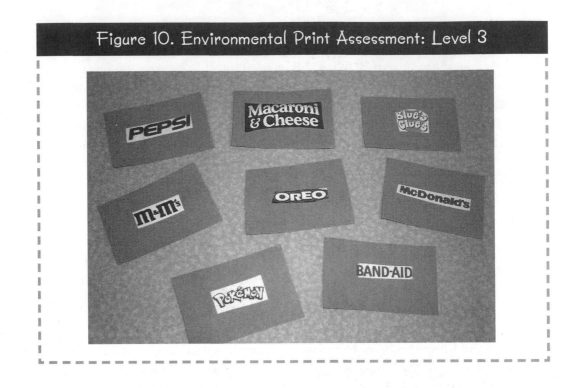

Figure 10. Environmental Print Assessment: Level 3

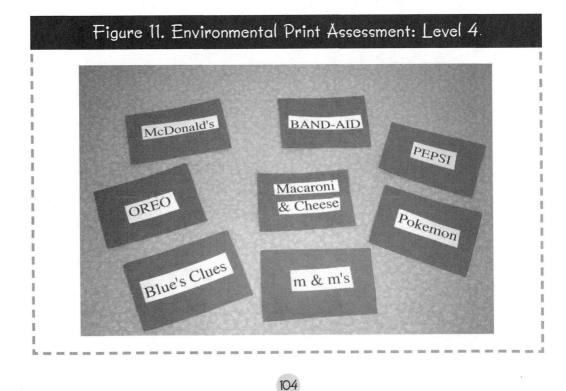

Figure 11. Environmental Print Assessment: Level 4

Figure 12. Environmental Print Reading Test Score Sheet

Child's Name_____

Child's Age in Months_____

☐ girl   ☐ boy

Directions: In the first column, list the 10 items you have selected to use for the Environmental Print Reading Test. Then, show a child the items or cards that correspond with each level of the test. The child should receive 2 points for each correct response, 1 point for a category response (e.g., soda for Pepsi), and 0 points for no response or an incorrect response. Total the number of points in each column.

Environmental Print Item	Level 1	Level 2	Level 3	Level 4
Total Points				

Using the Environmental Print Reading Test

Administer the Environmental Print Reading Test in a setting that is as free from distractions as possible. The test is best given to the individual child one on one. Levels 2 through 4 should be approached in a playful, card game format. These levels should be administered after the real items have been removed from the child's field of vision. A learning effect from Level 1 can change the scores on these subsequent levels of the test. Scoring of the test should follow these guidelines: Two points are given for correct reading of the logo, and one point is awarded for responses with meaningful words that include comprehension of categories. For example, a response of "soda" for a brand name cola product would be awarded 1 point for having abstracted the item to the level of its meaning category; no points would be awarded for wrong response or no response. Five consecutive miscues at any level are sufficient to indicate frustration, and testing should be discontinued.

Young children who often have difficulty focusing during other assessments find the Environmental Print Reading Test highly engaging. Real, high-profile items capture children's interest and ensure initial reading success because of their visual power. The card game format of the test contributes to maintaining a high-interest level. The test is short because it is based on 10 items, but the results demonstrate much about a child's prior experiences with print, letter recognition, and progression in early reading. Retesting at a later date documents growth and progress toward reading decontextualized words.

Observing Literacy Development

Reading and writing can develop naturally for children in a literate environment through playful exploration with literacy materials supported by interested, significant adults. Literacy development is the outgrowth of the same drives to communicate and express thinking that urge oral language and pictorial expression. Simply filling an early childhood setting or a kindergarten classroom with environmental print materials does not ensure that connections will be made and that experimentation with reading and writing will occur. Teachers need to be careful observers and recorders of what children do with literacy materials, including environmental print. Facilitating learning and instructional planning for children emerges from these observations.

Systematic observation of children's use of environmental print literacy materials has important advantages and functions in the early childhood setting. It allows the teacher to take an in-depth look at the child as he or she constructs understandings in a literacy act. Observation focuses on the child's natural literacy behaviors in an unobtrusive manner. Building on a child's strengths becomes the focus as the teacher notes what a child *can* do. Rich information becomes available from observations for the teacher, staff, and parents to evaluate program effectiveness, curriculum decisions, and individual progress.

Collecting Observational Data

Collecting and recording observational data as children use literacy materials and environmental print activities may include a number of useful methods. Narratives, sampling, and checklists all serve differing roles and functions in data collection.

Narratives

Narratives of children as they use environmental print play props, games, and learning activities can be made using an anecdotal record format. Anecdotal records are brief written accounts describing the play frame or literacy activity. The anecdote describes the behavior of the children in the incident in an objective manner, explaining the how, when, and where of the literacy activity. Anecdotal records are brief descriptions of short periods of time that become cumulative over time. They require little preparation and virtually no special training to conduct. Anecdotes are open-ended with no expected outcome and no single expected literacy activity as the topic. Unexpected, unanticipated events can be captured and recorded for interpretation at a later time. However, anecdotal records are certainly incomplete glimpses of the events in early childhood classrooms. The events, which capture the observers, are the ones that are recorded. Interpretation of the meaning behind the events is based on a small bit of information and is out of the literacy context.

With these cautions, a sample format for recording anecdotal notes is offered in Figure 13a. Figure 13b shows a completed version of the anecdotal record. The suggested format allows for interpretive comments next to the observed events. When observing children engaged on literacy play with environmental print materials, watch for the unusual and extraordinary ways children invent uses for the items. Observable behaviors to look for in anecdotal notes include the following:

Phonemic Awareness
- Can hear and pronounce sounds of English in environmental print play
- Can hear and stretch the letter sounds in logo words
- Can hear the word breaks in multiple word logos

Figure 13a. Anecdotal Record

Child's Name _____ Age _____

Observer _____ Date _____

Time _____ Place Observation Made _____

Incident	Comment

Figure 13b. Completed Anecdotal Record

Child's Name _Cesar_   Age _5_

Observer _Miss D._   Date _2003_

Time _10:00am_   Place Observation Made _ELL Classroom_

Incident	Comment
Four kindergartners are playing Bingo with the environmental print Bingo game. The children are playing with the colored logo cards. Cesar is the Bingo caller and stands and rocks back and forth as he calls the names of the logos.	This is high success engagement for Cesar. Sitting still to play is a challenge for him. Typically he has a low success rate with other kinds of reading. The next Bingo game should use black and white logos and students are capable of playing two cards at once to increase the challenge.

Letter Sound
- Recognizes the visual form and names the letters within the logo
- Identifies initial consonants
- Identifies ending consonants
- Identifies vowels within word
- Identifies rhyming words in logos
- Copies logos in writing

Concepts About Print
- Points out words/letters in logos
- Has one-to-one correspondence of words in environmental print
- Follows environmental print left to right, top to bottom

Another form of narrative data collection is the event record (see Figure 14a and b). It is a detailed account written in narrative as an event happens. The observer writes down everything that occurs at a particular place, with a particular activity, or with a specific child in a predetermined time period. The event record includes all events, dialogue, and behaviors, not just selected events as with the anecdotal record. Event records are necessarily short and use brief words to keep up with the stream of events and the pace of the action in the classroom. Using judgmental, descriptive words when recording is a danger in writing event records. It is a full, rich description of classroom events as they occur that is not limited to any one type of incident. Like the anecdotal note, the event record is open-ended and can capture a wide range of life events with young children. It does not demand specialized observational skills, just care in word choice. However, event records are very time consuming, require periods of uninterrupted observation, and are inefficient when there are large numbers of children involved with literacy play.

Sampling

Another way to observe children is through sampling certain occurrences and behaviors. Time sampling records the frequency with which an event occurs. A time sampling of literacy acts records how often children voluntarily use environmental print materials, use materials in interactions with others, and use environmental print materials in a referential way. The observer must prepare ahead to look for and record on a predetermined time interval (see Figure 15).

Event sampling studies the conditions under which events occur. In event sampling the use of environmental print materials, the observer looks

14a. Event Record

Title of Event _____

Observer _____ Date _____

Time _____ Place Observation Made _____

Observations | **Comment**

Figure 14b. Completed Event Record

Title of Event _Teacher-Facilitated Activity_

Observer _Mrs. J_   Date _2003_

Time _9:25 am_   Place Observation Made _Kindergarten classroom_

Observations	Comment
One group of children was working with the instructional assistant on the Food/Fun activity. In turn, the children grabbed a logo from the basket, determined the category, and then placed the logo on the chart. The assistant had the kids read the logos and the letters. "How do you know it's Corn Flakes?" "It has a chicken on it." "How do you know it says Pepsi?" "It starts with P."	The children seemed to be excited when they recognized logos.

Figure 15. Time Sampling Recording Sheet

Time Sampling
Event Frequency Recording

Directions: Every five minutes during a free play period, check for engagement with print materials. Use a hash mark across a number to indicate the frequency of engagement during a one-hour play period.

| 1 | 2 | 3 | 4 | 5 | 6 | 7 | 8 | 9 | 10 | 11 | 12 |

for the play that leads into the engagement with the materials, and what follows the play.

Sampling allows the teacher to evaluate how integral the environmental print materials are to literacy play and how engaged children are in using the materials.

Checklists

Checklists are lists of specific tasks, traits, or behaviors, which the observer watches for and records. Checklists work best with specific, observable events that can be checked off the list. Checklists can be valuable tools for focusing attention on specific, important events and behaviors. A survey of the use of environmental print activities and the learning from them can be conducted most efficiently using checklists.

A number of checklists have been developed to accompany the use of environmental print as a purposeful teaching tool in the early years setting. Some of the checklists are developed for use with just one child (see Figure 16). Others can be used by many different observers over time to acquire cumulative data. Finally, some checklists serve as data regarding the whole class.

Other Data

Parental evaluation data is essential to the assessment process as well. You can use the Parent Questionnaire (see Figure 17) to gather information from parents as they notice changing print awareness at home.

Figure 16. Knowledge of Sounds and Letters Checklist

Student's Name_____ Date _____

Directions: As the student is working with environmental print games and activities, cross through the letters he or she recognizes in a logo. If a letter sound also is recognized in the logo, mark it for sound recognition □.

F □	K □	I □	T □	C □
O □	X □	A □	G □	U □
Z □	P □	J □	V □	Q □
B □	R □	L □	M □	D □
N □	W □	S □	E □	Y □
H □				
f □	k □	i □	t □	c □
o □	x □	a □	g □	u □
z □	p □	j □	v □	q □
b □	r □	l □	m □	d □
n □	w □	s □	e □	y □
h □	ch □	th □	sh □	

Total Uppercase_____/sounds____
Total Lowercase_____/sounds____

Figure 17. Parent Questionnaire

1. Describe what you have noticed about your child's recognition of letters in the community.

_____

_____

_____

_____

_____

2. Has your child told you about environmental print activities in school? Explain.

_____

_____

_____

_____

_____

3. Have you heard your child identify or discuss logos or other print in the environment? Please describe.

_____

_____

_____

_____

_____

_____

4. Have you engaged in any environmental print reading activities at home or in the community? Please describe.

_____

_____

_____

_____

_____

5. What is your opinion about the use of familiar logos and print in the environment to teach beginning reading skills?

_____

_____

_____

_____

_____

_____

The primary function of literacy assessment in the early years is to determine what each child is able to do and how he or she is progressing. Ongoing assessment helps instruction to be closely attuned to what children need next in the teaching–learning cycle. In all the examples offered here, the teacher is the instrument of assessment. Careful observation offers strong data for teacher planning and decision making.

In chapter 6, we share recommendations for teachers who wish to implement an environmental print curriculum. And, because families are such an important part of the instruction–assessment cycle, we also include activities for reinforcement experiences at home.

CHAPTER 6

Getting Started: Recommendations for Teachers and Parents

That is what learning is. You suddenly understand something you've understood all your life, but in a new way.

DORIS LESSING (AS CITED IN MAGGIO, 1997, P. 62)

As we conducted our research, we felt it was important to meet with teachers and discuss their thoughts about the effectiveness of environmental print for beginning reading instruction. In addition, we also conducted a survey as another means for teachers to share their thoughts, successes, and suggestions (see Appendix B for survey and survey results). Through our discussions with teachers, we have gained greater insight into the success teachers and students have experienced with environmental print. For example, while reflecting with the teachers participating in the studies, one kindergarten teacher mentioned that she felt the success of the environmental print curriculum was largely due to the environment's constant reinforcement of classroom instruction and activities (personal communication, November 14, 2002). She believed that, while it is often difficult to enlist the help of parents to reinforce skills learned at school, an environment filled with meaningful print became that needed reinforcement for the children. Rather than looking at a McDonald's sign and thinking just about hamburgers, children were, instead, reminded of their literacy instruction in school. This teacher felt that her students had a better grasp of letters and sounds because of the ongoing, high-profile reinforcement beyond the classroom walls.

As a result of the data we have gathered through our research, it is clearer to us now that environmental print has been overlooked in intentional instruction and as curriculum materials that build awareness of print, concepts about print, and the conventions of written language. Environmental print has been an invisible bridge between emergent reading and alphabetic decoding. Print in the real world—the signs, billboards, logos, and functional print that saturate a child's environment in a literate society—passively communicates many literacy lessons to children. As teachers, we can actively and creatively apply those lessons in our classrooms to help children connect sounds to letters.

Creating an environmental print curriculum and enriching an existing instructional program need not be complicated or time-consuming. Materials for creating the activities are as near as the cupboard or the newspaper. Systematic assessment of how and when children use the environmental print curriculum informs and guides instruction. What each child knows about print and needs to learn next becomes clear as assessment documents the stages of growth in literacy.

Recommendations for Teachers

We offer the following recommendations to teachers who wish to implement an environmental print curriculum.

- Become familiar with the things that are relevant in children's lives in order to adequately motivate them to learn to read. Use the environmental print that is familiar to students to create games and activities that draw attention to beginning letters in logos and the sounds they make.

- Stock play centers with props that are familiar and functional. Environmental print props, such as fast-food bags, pizza boxes, milk cartons, and cereal boxes enrich classroom sociodramatic play centers.

- Be aware of children's functional knowledge of print. By using a testing instrument such as the Environmental Print Reading Test described in chapter 5, you can gain greater insight to children's awareness of the print in their environment.

Making the Home–School Connection

Parents can become involved in school literacy experiences at home as well. The family serves as the child's most important teacher by providing first experiences with print and literacy materials. Home language and the presence of text in the family environment is the beginning place of literacy. Literacy materials are readily available in the products and packaging children see at home and in their neighborhoods. Environmental print is familiar text for most children regardless of context or circumstance. Parents can assist their children in learning to read by using simple and fun activities. Teachers can provide these activities for parents or send them home with students as homework. We suggest the following activities.

Reading Real Objects. When playing house, grocery store, or restaurant, parents can allow children to use real objects such as drink bottles, milk cartons, cookie and cereal boxes, restaurant bags, and take-out menus. While children are playing, parents can encourage their children to notice print and name the logo or food on the container.

Puzzles. Parents can create simple puzzles with their children by cutting apart cardboard packaging from cereal boxes, detergent boxes, soda cartons, and so forth. Parents should work with their children to discuss the puzzles as they are assembled.

Shopping Trip. Encourage parents to assist with locating favorite items at the store. While grocery shopping, ask children to help you find the items on the grocery list. You will be surprised at how many items they recognize. Use the hunt for items as an opportunity to read labels and name letters with children. Have children match coupons and shopping list items to the products on the grocery shelves.

On the Road. Driving time can become a quality time for parents to point out signs and billboards to their children. Encourage parents to draw attention to words and letters and ask their children to identify the ones they notice. For example, a parent might say, "I spy a *T*." The child looks around to locate a *T* in the environment.

Walks. On walks and outings, parents can point out signs and billboards and ask their children what a word says, or they can read aloud the word together.

As we reflect on the children who have participated in our studies, we are reminded of smiling faces and enthusiastic comments. It is our belief that children respond so favorably because a part of their world is acknowledged at school. Items that typically have home or life significance are valued and used as a basis for school instruction. The children are not only given the opportunity to participate in enjoyable, motivating, and meaningful activities that positively impact their print awareness and sound identification but also they are exposed to an enormous literacy resource that is all around them— their world.

Description of Authors' Studies

Study 1: Teaching Beginning Reading Skills With Environmental Print

The first study was conducted to determine the effectiveness of environmental print in the form of instructional materials in kindergartners' development of letter–sound recognition and the ability to read environmental print logos in differing decontextualized forms. Another purpose was to determine whether or not letter–sound recognition and the ability to read environmental print would increase with teacher-facilitated instruction. The third purpose was to examine the role of socioeconomic status (SES) in the development of print awareness, letter recognition, and sound identification with the use of environmental print. The study was conducted in both higher and lower socioeconomic areas. Socioeconomic status was determined by the number of children receiving free and reduced lunch as well as by the average family income for the area. Six all-day kindergarten classrooms participated as follows.

Treatment Group 1: Seventeen kindergarten children at the lower SES school and 17 kindergarten children at the higher SES school used environmental print materials (games, puzzles, books) in centers. They also experienced two teacher-facilitated lessons each week, focusing on the sounds and letters in environmental print logos. This group is referred to as the teacher-facilitated group throughout the study.

Treatment Group 2: Twenty kindergarten children at a lower SES school and 21 kindergarten children at a higher SES school used environmental print materials in centers. They did not receive teacher-facilitated lessons with environmental print. This group is referred to as the indirect-instruction group throughout the study.

Control Group: Sixteen kindergarten children at a lower SES school and 16 kindergarten children at a higher SES school were not exposed systematically or intentionally to environmental print activities or instruction in the classroom. The control classes in this study were conducted in a similar manner to the teacher-facilitated instruction and indirect instruction classes. Instruction was organized in learning-center format with a teacher instructing one group, an instructional aide instructing another group, and other groups working independently. These classrooms, similar to the treatment classrooms, were highly academic with a great deal of attention focused on the instruction of letters and sounds.

All children in the study were assessed with three pretests—Alphabet Recognition, Letter–Sound Recognition, and Environmental Print Reading Test (described in chapter 5).

Procedure

The study began the week after pretesting. Both the teacher-directed and indirect instruction groups in each SES school received a set of games and puzzles (described in chapter 3). In order to encourage and maintain student interest, all the experimental classes (both teacher-facilitated and indirect instruction) received two or three new games and puzzles each week. The teachers had the students use these materials two times a week at a learning center for approximately 15 minutes. During this time, the children used the games independently. Teacher involvement was limited to explaining the activities and how to use the materials, and answering specific questions asked by the children. The teachers in Treatment Group 1 received two activities to teach or facilitate each week (described in chapter 2). All the teacher-facilitated activities involved discussion, not only of the logos themselves, but also of the letters used in the logo words and the sounds they represent.

Observations of Teacher-Directed and Independent Activities

Weekly observations were performed and field notes recorded in each of the treatment and control classrooms in all three schools for the following purposes:

- To maintain the integrity of the study (prevent contamination, ensure proper use of the materials, etc.).
- To identify whether teacher-facilitated instruction and indirect instruction models were performed consistently as anticipated.
- To identify how children were utilizing and responding to the materials and instruction.

Data Analysis

Pretest and posttest measures were collected for environmental print recognition, alphabet letter recognition, and knowledge of letter sounds. Analysis was performed using one-tailed t tests (to determine overall gains), one-way ANOVAs (to determine differences between treatment groups), and two-way ANOVAs (to determine differences between SES groups).

Results

Results of this study (see Table 1) revealed that kindergartners' print awareness increased with the use of environmental print materials, and that the addition of

Table 1. Lower SES Group

Treatment Group	n	L1-Pre		L1-Post		L2-Pre		L2-Post	
		M	SD	M	SD	M	SD	M	SD
Focused Instruction	17	11.7	3.3	15.05	2.1	10.9	3.4	15.2	1.9
Indirect Instruction	20	10.8	4.3	12.3	3.8	10.9	4.1	12.4	3.6
Control	16	9.3	4.4	9.5	4.2	8.8	4.5	10.1	4.2

Treatment Group	n	L3-Pre		L3-Post		L4-Pre		L4-Post	
		M	SD	M	SD	M	SD	M	SD
Focused Instruction	17	5.05	3.4	15	2.1	.58	1.2	10.3	4.2
Indirect Instruction	20	3.7	3.7	8.2	4.4	.05	.22	2.6	3.5
Control	16	4.9	4.9	6.5	4.0	.62	1.9	1.6	2.8

Treatment Group	n	Letter-Pre		Letter-Post		Sound-Pre		Sound-Post	
		M	SD	M	SD	M	SD	M	SD
Focused Instruction	17	4.2	6.5	18	8.5	.82	3	16.6	8.1
Indirect Instruction	20	1.8	2.6	15.3	11.6	1.5	2.5	9.6	10.2
Control	16	5.7	8.1	17.5	8.5	1.8	4.9	9.93	8.0

Higher SES Group

Treatment Group	n	L1-Pre		L1-Post		L2-Pre		L2-Post	
		M	SD	M	SD	M	SD	M	SD
Focused Instruction	17	14	1.8	15.9	.24	14	2.2	15.5	1.3
Indirect Instruction	21	14.6	2.2	15.1	1.6	13.5	2.8	15	1.9
Control	16	15.06	.92	15.06	1.1	14.8	1.04	14.6	1.9

Treatment Group	n	L3-Pre		L3-Post		L4-Pre		L4-Post	
		M	SD	M	SD	M	SD	M	SD
Focused Instruction	17	8.4	3.9	15.5	1.1	3.1	3.9	12.05	3.8
Indirect Instruction	21	8.3	3.7	11.9	3.7	1.4	2.6	6.0	4.8
Control	16	9.25	2.6	9.9	2.4	2.4	2.8	4.4	3.6

Treatment Group	n	Letter-Pre		Letter-Post		Sound-Pre		Sound-Post	
		M	SD	M	SD	M	SD	M	SD
Focused Instruction	17	16	9.1	24.6	2.0	9.5	9.9	20.9	3.9
Indirect Instruction	21	17.2	7.9	22.9	5.2	7.8	9.3	16.9	7.5
Control	16	13.5	10.6	22.4	4.0	6.06	6.9	16.6	5.6

teacher-facilitated instruction brought about increased print awareness with children in both higher and lower SES schools. No significant differences existed in letter recognition. Sound identification results were divided according to SES group. At the lower SES school, teacher-facilitated instruction brought about the greatest improvements. With the higher SES classes, no significant difference existed between groups. Socioeconomic status was found to have played a role in the effectiveness of instruction concerning print awareness. Both experimental classes at the lower SES school showed improvement on all but one level of the Environmental Print Reading Test. The greatest improvement took place in the teacher-facilitated instruction class. The socioeconomic area seemed to play a role in letter recognition, as all kindergartners at the high SES school experienced significant increases, suggesting that environmental print did not bring about these results. No significant differences were revealed between socioeconomic groups concerning sound identification. The most obvious difference existed between classes within the lower SES school. The teacher-facilitated instruction class experienced greater improvement over both the indirect instruction and control groups. This suggests that the difference in sound identification is attributed to instructional style.

This study revealed that environmental print is an effective tool for teaching beginning reading skills when attention is drawn to the letters in the logos and the sounds the letters make. By creating games that drew attention to the letters and through teacher-facilitated activities, the children began to recognize that these meaningful pictures contained letters and the letters made the sounds they hear in the logos. The results of the study suggest that adult interaction with environmental print materials is particularly successful in assisting children in making the transition from seeing logos as merely graphics to seeing them as graphics that contain letters and words.

Study 2: Comparison of Environmental Print Reading in Three Schools

In this study, 36 children in three early kindergarten classrooms were given the Environmental Print Reading Test. Early kindergarten is defined as children who turn 5 years old between September and December of the school year, thereby, missing the state age cutoff for public kindergarten attendance. The mean age for the children participating was 5 years, 3 months. The classrooms were located at three differing school sites. Site 1 is a middle income, predominantly white suburb of a large metropolitan area. Families of the students at this site might be characterized as intact, two-parent, and professional. Twenty-nine percent of the population of the school is diverse, with free and reduced lunches at 32%.

The second site is located in a declining, lower income, working-class area of the same metropolitan area. A large number of multifamily housing units are located within the school boundaries. Homes surrounding the school are 20 to 30 years old. Many of the families of the students at this site are single-parent and grandparent heads of households. There is an even greater level of diversity at this school. Free and reduced lunches at this site are at 39%.

The third site is one of the oldest schools in the school district of the metropolitan area. Eighty-seven percent of the students attending the school are on free or reduced lunches. The site is a Title I school with 60% of the families around the school living below the federal poverty level. A transient population from nearby motel and homeless shelters attends the school.

Results

The results on initial reading of environmental print using the Environmental Print Reading Test (see Table 2) demonstrates the differing results obtained in comparing diverse communities. The test score means and standard deviation

Table 2. Environmental Print Reading Test Results			
Test Level 1	n	M	SD
Site 1	11	14.45	0.82
Site 2	14	13.79	0.97
Site 3	11	16.50	0.93
Test Level 2	n	M	SD
Site 1	11	12.36	4.34
Site 2	14	12.43	2.47
Site 3	11	15.40	2.06
Test Level 3	n	M	SD
Site 1	11	9.09	4.44
Site 2	14	5.86	2.11
Site 3	11	11.60	8.35
Test Level 4	n	M	SD
Site 1	11	5.09	5.80
Site 2	14	1.93	2.23
Site 3	11	3.80	2.25

of scores on this reading test suggest that children in the high need, urban core areas read environmental print more readily than their counterparts in lower income and middle class areas. Not only did children at Site 3 read environmental print better on real items at Level 1 of the reading test, but also they continued to read decontextualized print better than their counterparts at the other two sites. At Level 4 of the test, where print is completely decontextualized without any context clues, performance in reading of environmental print dropped significantly.

Not surprisingly, a scan of the types and quality of print surrounding Site 3 reveals that print is more dense, directional in nature, and highly commercial. However, in the middle class neighborhood, Site 1, there are no advertising billboards and environmental print is infrequent, functional, and more aesthetically tasteful. Children growing up in urban core areas are immersed in environmental print. Advertising through mainstream print media is much less successful here. Environmental print that is commercial is often the only form of print children living in urban areas may see in their day-to-day lives away from school. This is one of the multiple literacies that children in an urban area bring to school literacy and must be utilized to help each child to learn to read successfully.

Study 3: Meaningful Connections to Read With English Language Learning Kindergartners

Does the use of environmental print materials influence print awareness, phonemic awareness, and phonological awareness in kindergartners learning English as their second language? This study was conducted with two small groups of kindergarten students learning English in a pull-out model of English-language learning (ELL). The study site was an elementary school in a large western metropolitan area with a mixture of low-, middle-, and high-income families. The student population was relatively diverse with 32% free and reduced lunches.

Method

The treatment group of five morning kindergarten children in the ELL program used environmental print materials including games, puzzles, books, and play props as enrichment to their typical ELL curriculum. The children received a minimum of two teacher-directed lessons each week using the environmental print materials. These lessons direct attention to specific letters and sounds in the environmental print words. The control group of six afternoon kindergarten children who were not exposed to the environmental print materials or activities received the unmodified, typical ELL curriculum.

The study was originally intended to span 15 weeks of instruction, but it was concluded at the end of 12 weeks.

Results

Both groups of ELL students increased letter-sound recognition by the end of the study; however, it is notable that the experimental group was able to identify lowercase letters and their sounds with greater frequency when compared to the control group.

The results (see Table 3) with this admittedly small sample of English-language learners are promising. The experimental group was reading print from logos used in the environmental print activities in a decontextualized manner at the conclusion of the study while the control group was not.

The results do indicate that environmental print as enrichment to direct instruction methods creates an effective bridge to English written language with a high rate of success. The study confirmed that literacy first is highly contextualized, visual learning. Children newly arrived in our market-driven society, are "captured" by high-profile logos and are compelled to read their messages.

The teachers, with more that 30 years combined teaching experience, recognized in the early weeks of the study that environmental print and the types of activities developed by the researchers was significantly enhancing language acquisition for the morning students. These teachers personally struggled with "shortchanging" their afternoon English-language learners. To maintain the integrity of the study, the teachers did not use any environmental print activities with the afternoon students and felt these children were lagging too far behind the morning group. So that she could begin using the environmental print enrichment activities with the afternoon class, the study was concluded early.

Table 3. Test Results

Alphabet Knowledge Test Results: Control Group

Pretest	Posttest	
	Uppercase	Lowercase
0	9	2
0	0	0
13	16	16
0	Dropped out of study	
0	Dropped out of study	

Alphabet Knowledge Test Results: Experimental Group

Pretest	Posttest	
	Uppercase	Lowercase
0	0	0
0	14	0
0	8	5
0	8	9
0	4	2
0	Dropped out of study	

Environmental Print Test Results: Control Group

	Pretest				Posttest			
Level	1	2	3	4	1	2	3	4
	14	14	6	0	Dropped out of study			
	6	6	0	0	10	0	2	0
	14	14	4	0	17	15	10	0
	7	6	0	0	18	15	0	0
	4	0	0	0	3	0		
	12	13	12	0	Dropped out of study			

No decontextualized reading of words at the end of the study.

Environmental Print Test Results: Experimental Group

	Pretest				Posttest			
Level	1	2	3	4	1	2	3	4
	15	0	0	0	20	20	20	16
	13	14	10	0	18	19	18	8
	18	16	13	0	20	20	20	16
	19	19	12	0	Dropped out of study			

From no reading to reading decontextualized print 40–80% of the time.

Survey and Survey Results

The following are teacher reflections from a survey about the implementation of environmental print instructional activities.

What were your observations about how the children used and/or enjoyed the environmental print games and activities?

"The students enjoyed the games and were very focused on letters and sounds during these activities."

"The children felt comfortable and successful using familiar logos in games and activities."

Were there any games and/or activities that the children particularly liked?

"Memory and matching games."

"The board game with the spinner."

"They seemed to like them all, but they really liked the memory games."

Were there any games and/or activities that the children did not seem to enjoy?

"No."

"They didn't seem too interested in just the books where there was no interacting."

In reference to previous school years, did you notice any difference in the children's abilities to identify sounds and letters?

"Yes. The students seem to be more aware of letters in their environment."

Did you receive comments from parents that pertained to the use of environmental print (noticing print or letters in the environment, etc.)?

"Parents have commented on how their child is reading letters everywhere they go and saying things like, 'Mom, you hear /t/-/t/-/t/-Target.'"

"Parents communicated comments, such as,

- 'At Wal-Mart my child was excited when he could spell the letters in logos.'
- 'My child is much more observant of street signs.'
- 'My child read all the boxes of cereal in our pantry.'"

If you were to continue to use these activities in future years, would you do anything differently?

"Just do more of it!"

"Introduce printed words at the very first with logo. Encourage matching of logos to words because the font used in logos is so different as each logo was introduced. Use fewer logos, concentrating on each one."

"I would want to be more involved with the children when they used environmental print."

Do you think you will use environmental print in this way in the future?

"Yes. The students' interest is there because the activities involve things that the students know and they are noticing that letters and sounds are everywhere—not just at school."

"I am going to use the environmental print activities next year. I will use the teacher-directed activities rather than just independent games for the students."

What other comments would you like to share?

"My students really enjoyed the activities and the variety of activities. I think tying the environmental print to the study of letters and sounds increases the students' awareness of their surroundings."

"I realized that my students were enjoying making up their own games with the environmental print activities."

"I thought that this was an excellent study. It was exciting for me to see my students' excitement when they could tell me a logo."

"I think environmental print is a great instructional tool."

"Great idea to see how environmental print would affect phonetic sounds/recognition. It made lessons fun and exciting and provided for additional activities to review lessons taught."

"The children had a lot of fun with the materials. I had never thought of using environmental print in this way, so I'm looking forward to doing more of it in the future."

REFERENCES

Aldridge, J., & Rust, D. (1987). A beginning reading strategy. *Academic Therapy, 22*(3), 323–326.

Anderson, G., & Markle, A. (1985). Cheerios, McDonald's and Snickers: Bringing EP into the classroom. *Reading Education in Texas, 1*, 30–35.

Bergen, D. (Ed.). (1988). *Play as a medium for learning and development*. Portsmouth, NH: Heinemann.

Block, C.C. (1993). Strategy instruction in a literature-based reading program. *The Elementary School Journal, 94*(2), 139–151.

Cazden, C.B. (1974). Play with language and metalinguistic awareness: One dimension of language experience. *Urban Review, 7*(1), 28–39.

Christie, J.F., Enz, B.J., Han, M., Gerard, M., Prior, J., Foley, D., et al. (2001). *Environmental print: An assessment instrument and instructional activities*. Paper presented at the Arizona State University Language and Literacy Conference, Tempe.

Christie, J.F., Enz, B.J., Gerard, M., & Prior, J. (2002, May). *Using environmental print as teaching materials and assessment tools*. Paper presented at the 47th Annual Convention of the International Reading Association, San Francisco, CA.

Christie, J.F., Enz, B.J., Gerard, M., Han, M., & Prior, J. (2003a, April). *Examining the instructional uses of environmental print*. Paper presented at the 48th Annual Convention of the International Reading Association, Orlando, FL.

Christie, J.F., Enz, B.J., Gerard, M., Han, M., & Prior, J. (2003b, December). *Understanding how environmental print supports early literacy*. Paper presented at the 53rd annual meeting of the National Reading Conference, Scottsdale, AZ.

Christie, J.F., Enz, B., & Vukelich, C. (2002). *Teaching language and literacy: Preschool through the elementary grades*. New York: Longman.

Cloer, T., Aldridge, J., & Dean, R. (1981/1982). Examining different levels of print awareness. *Journal of Language Experience, 4*(1 & 2), 25–33.

Entwisle, D.R. (1995). The role of schools in sustaining early childhood program benefits. *Future of Children, 5*(3), 133–144.

Enz, B., & Christie, J.F. (1997). Teacher play interaction styles: Effects on play behavior and relationships with teacher training and experience. *International Journal of Early Childhood Education, 2*, 55–69.

Fein, G.G. (1981). Pretend play in childhood: An integrative review. *Child Development, 52*(4), 1095–1118.

Ferreiro, E., & Teberosky, A. (1982). *Literacy before schooling*. Exeter, NH: Heinemann.

Froebel, F. (1902). *Education of man* (W.H. Hailman, Trans.). New York: Appleton. (Original work published 1826)

Gleason, J.B. (1966). Do children imitate? *Proceedings of the International Conference on Oral Education of the Deaf, 2*, 441–448.

Goodman, K. (1970). Reading: A psycholinguistic guessing game. In H. Singer & R.B. Ruddell (Eds.), *Theoretical models and processes of reading* (pp. 259–271). Newark, DE: International Reading Association.

Harste, J., Burke, C., & Woodward, V. (1982). Children's language and world: Initial encounters with print. In J.A. Langer & M.T. Smith-Burke (Eds.), *Reader meets author/bridging the gap: A psycholinguistic and sociolinguistic perspective* (pp. 105–131). Newark, DE: International Reading Association.

International Reading Association. (1999). *High stakes assessments in reading*. A position statement of the International Reading Association. Newark, DE: Author.

Isenberg, J.P., & Jalongo, M. (1993). *Creative expression and play in the early childhood curriculum*. New York: Merrill.

Johnson, J.E., Christie, J.F., & Yawkey, T.D. (1999). *Play and early childhood development* (2nd ed.). Glenview, IL: Scott, Foresman.

Kuby, P. (1994). *Early reading ability of kindergarten children following environmental print instructions*. Unpublished doctoral dissertation, The University of Alabama at Birmingham.

Kuby, P., & Aldridge, J. (1997). Direct versus indirect environmental print instruction and early reading ability in kindergarten children. *Reading Psychology: International Quarterly, 18*(2), 91–104.

Kuby, P., Aldridge, J., & Snyder, S. (1994). Developmental progression of environmental print recognition in kindergarten children. *Reading Psychology: International Quarterly, 15*(1), 1–9.

Maggio, R. (1997). *Quotations on education*. Paramus, NJ: Prentice Hall.

Masonheimer, P., Drum, P., & Ehri, L. (1984). Does environmental print identification lead children into word reading? *Journal of Reading Behavior, 16*(4), 257–271.

Morrow, L. (1989, December). *Preparing the classroom environment to promote literacy during play*. Paper presented at the 39th annual meeting of the National Reading Conference, Austin, TX.

National Institute of Child Health and Human Development. (2002). *Report of the National Reading Panel. Teaching children to read: An evidence-based assessment of the scientific research literature on reading and its implications for reading instruction* (NIH Publication No. 00-4769). Washington, DC: U.S. Government Printing Office.

National Association for the Education of Young Children. (2001, September). What does it look like and what does it take? Supporting early literacy. *Young Children, 56*(5), 56–57.

Neill, S. (1982). Experimental alterations in playroom layout and their effect on staff and child behavior. *Education Psychology, 2*, 103–119.

Neuman, S.B., & Roskos, K. (1990). Play, print, and purpose: Enriching play environments for literacy development. *The Reading Teacher, 44*, 214–221.

Neuman, S.B., & Roskos, K. (1993). Access to print for children of poverty: Differential effects of adult mediation and literacy-enriched play settings on environmental print and functional print tasks. *American Educational Research Journal, 30*(1), 95–122.

No Child Left Behind Act of 2001, Pub. L. No. 107-110, 115 Stat. 1425 (2003).

Orellana, M.F., & Hernandez, A. (2003). Talking the walk: Children reading urban environmental print. In P.A. Mason & J.S. Schumm (Eds.), *Promising practices for urban reading instruction* (pp. 25–36). Newark, DE: International Reading Association.

Pellegrini, A.D. (1985). The relations between symbolic play and literate behavior: A review and critique of the empirical literature. *Review Educational Research, 55*(1), 107–121.

Piaget, J. (1962). *Play, dreams and imitation in childhood* (C. Garregno & F.M. Hodgson, Trans.). New York: Norton. (Original work published 1951)

Pressley, M.C., Rankin, J., & Yokoi, Y. (1996). A survey of instructional practices of primary teachers nominated as effective in promoting literacy. *The Elementary School Journal, 96*(4), 363–384.

Prior, J. (2003). *Environmental print: Meaningful connections for learning to read*. Unpublished doctoral dissertation, Arizona State University, Tempe.

Ratcliff, N. (2001). Use the environment to prevent discipline problems and support learning. *Young Children, 56*(5), 84–88.

Roskos, K.A., Christie, J.F., & Richgels, D.J. (2003). The essentials of early literacy instruction. *Young Children, 58*(2), 52–60.

Simmons, D., Gunn, B., Smith, S., & Kameenui, E.J. (1994). Phonological awareness: Application of instructional design. *LD Forum, 19*(2), 7–10.

Smith, S. (1996, December). *A longitudinal study: The literacy development of 57 children.* Paper presented at the 46th annual meeting of the National Reading Conference, Charleston, SC.

Trawick-Smith, J. (1998). A qualitative analysis of metaplay in the preschool years. *Early Childhood Research Quarterly, 13*(3), 433–452.

U.S. Department of Education. (2004). *Early reading first.* Retrieved June 21, 2004, from http://www.ed.gov/programs/earlyreading/index.html

Vygotsky, L.S. (1978). Play and its role in the mental development of the child. *Soviet Psychology, 12*(6), 62–76.

Ylisto, I. (1967). *An empirical investigation of early reading responses of young children.* Unpublished doctoral dissertation, University of Michigan, Ann Arbor.

INDEX

- - - - -

Note: Page numbers followed by *f* indicate figures.

A

ACTIVITIES. *See specific activities*
ACTIVITY EXTENSION, 23
AIRPORT/TRAVEL AGENT PROP BOX, 20*f*
ALDRIDGE, J., 5, 6, 7, 13, 102
ALPHABET KNOWLEDGE: ABC book for, 62–71; direct instruction for, 8–9; as predictor of reading proficiency, 6; teachers' modeling of, 25–26; word wall for, 55
ANDERSON, G., 4
ANECDOTAL RECORDS, 107–110
ANGELOU, M., 1
ART CENTER, 18
ASSESSMENT: assumptions of, 101–102; government recommendations for, 4; of independent games, 78*f*; purpose of, 101; types of, 101. *See also specific types*

B

BACKGROUND KNOWLEDGE, 2, 27
BEACH/OCEAN PROP BOX, 20*f*
BERGEN, D., 17
BIG BOOK, 34
BINGO, 72–73
BLOCK, C.C., 3
BOOKS, 17. *See also specific types*
BOOKSTORE CENTER, 15*f*
BURKE, C., 6, 7

C

CATEGORIZATION ACTIVITIES, 42–45, 47–49, 51–54. *See also* matching games
CAZDEN, C.B., 14
CEREAL BOX ACTIVITY, 85
CHECKLISTS, 113
CHRISTIE, J.F., 6, 7, 8, 20, 23, 25
CLASSROOM ORGANIZATION, 16–19
CLOER, T., 6, 7, 102
COGNITIVE DEVELOPMENT, 12
COLLAGES, 54

COMPREHENSION, 16

CONCENTRATION GAME, 79–80

CONSTRUCTION/GARAGE PROP BOX, 20*f*

CULTURE, 14

D

DEAN, R., 6, 7, 102

DECONTEXTUALIZED READING, 56

DEMONSTRATIONS, 22

DIRECT INSTRUCTION, 6, 8–9

DIRECTIONS, 22

DOCTOR PROP BOX, 20*f*

DRUM, P., 6

E

EARLY READING FIRST PROGRAM: assessment recommendations of, 4; environmental print recommendations of, 5; goals of, 1; literacy-rich environment definition of, 3; oral language definition of, 3

ECONOMICALLY DISADVANTAGED CHILDREN: print knowledge of, 4; studies with, 120–125; and teacher-as-facilitator approach, 8

EHRI, L., 6

ENGLISH LANGUAGE LEARNERS: direct instruction for, 8–9; letter recognition of, 9; studies with, 125–126, 127*t*

ENTWISLE, D.R., 4

ENVIRONMENTAL PRINT: booklet of, 35–37; children's interest in, 5; curriculum implementation for, 26–29; definition of, 1; function of, 4–5; gathering, 27–29; government recommendations for, 5; in home environment, 4; importance of, 5; as instructional tool, 7–9; in play, 13–16; as reading text, 5–7; research studies of, 7, 120–127; teaching strategies with, 19, 22–24

ENVIRONMENTAL PRINT READING TEST, 8, 102–106

ENZ, B.J., 7, 8, 23, 25

EVENT RECORDS, 110, 111*f*–114*f*

EXTENSION, ACTIVITY, 23

F

FAIRY TALE PROP BOX, 20*f*

FANTASY, 13

FARM PROP BOX, 20*f*

FAST-FOOD CENTER, 15*f*

FEEDBACK, 23

FEIN, G.G., 16

FLIP BOOKS, 88–90
FLOOR PLANS, 39–40
FOLEY, D., 7
FOOD LOGO ACTIVITY, 74–75, 84
FROEBEL, F., 11
FUNCTIONAL PRINT: big book of, 34; definition of, 4; importance of, 4–5

G

GAMES: adaptation of, 27; for independent play, 76–78; overview of, 24; for use by parents, 119; with and without direct instruction, 8–9. *See also specific types*
GERARD, M., 7, 8, 25
GLEASON, J.B., 14
GO FISH GAME, 87*f*
GOODMAN, K., 6
GRAPHS, 58*f*–61*f*
GROCERY STORE CENTER, 15*f*
GUNN, B., 2

H

HAN, M., 7, 8, 25
HARSTE, J., 6, 7
HERNANDEZ, A., 25, 101
HOME ENVIRONMENT: chart for, 39–40; environmental print in, 4; questionnaire regarding, 113–116
HOME LIVING CENTER, 13–14, 15*f*
HOME–SCHOOL CONNECTIONS, 3–4, 118–119

I

INDEPENDENT GAMES, 76–78. *See also specific games*
INFANTS, 14
INTERNATIONAL READING ASSOCIATION, 101
ISENBERG, J.P., 12

J

JALONGO, M., 12
JOHNSON, J.E., 20

K

KAMEENUI, E.J., 2
KINDERGARTEN PROGRAMS, 3
KUBY, P., 5, 7, 13

L

LABELING OBJECTS, 22
LANGUAGE: function of, 11–12; in play, 15–16; play with, 14–15
LANGUAGE ENVIRONMENT, 3
LANGUAGE LEARNING, 3
LEARNING CENTERS, 13–16, 17
LESSING, D., 117
LETTER COLLAGES, 54
LETTER, PARENT, 30*f*
LETTER RECOGNITION, 2, 9
LETTER SORTING, 91–94
LIBRARY CENTER, 15*f*, 17
LITERACY-RICH ENVIRONMENT, 3
LOGOS: ABC book for, 62–71; bingo with, 72–73; book of, 31–33, 35–37; categorization activities for, 42–45, 47–49, 51–54; children's distinguishing between, 6; children's interest in, 5; children's interpretation of, 7; collection tips for, 27, 29; creating assessment instrument with, 102–106; decontextualized reading with, 56; flip book with, 88–90; food activity with, 74–75, 84; go fish game with, 87; graphing of, 57–61; home chart of, 39–40; matching games with, 79–80, 86, 99; missing graphics activity with, 86; recognition game for, 35–37; sounding out activity for, 46; spinner game with, 95–97; two-letter folder activity with, 98

M

MAGGIO, R., 117
MAIL CENTER, 15*f*
MAKE-BELIEVE PLAY, 13, 15–16
MARKLE, A., 4
MASONHEIMER, P., 6
MATCHING GAMES, 79–80, 86, 91–94, 99. *See also* categorization activities
MEDIATION, 20
MODELING, 25–26
MORROW, L., 17
MOTIVATION, 12

N

NAME BOOKS, 71
NARRATIVE COMPETENCE, 16
NARRATIVES, 107–110
NATIONAL ASSOCIATION FOR THE EDUCATION OF YOUNG CHILDREN, 2
NATIONAL INSTITUTE OF CHILD HEALTH AND HUMAN DEVELOPMENT (NICHD), 1

NATIONAL READING PANEL, 1
NEIGHBORHOOD MAPS, 41
NEILL, S., 17
NEUMAN, S.B., 13, 17, 23
NO CHILD LEFT BEHIND LEGISLATION, 1

O

OBSERVATIONS, 106–116
OFFICE/WRITING CENTER, 15*f*
ORAL LANGUAGE, 2, 3
ORELLANA, M.F., 25, 101

P

PARENTS: activities for use by, 118–119; importance of, 25; letter for, 30*f*;
    questionnaire for, 115*f*; role of, in fostering children's interest, 5
PHONEMIC AWARENESS: definition of, 2; foundation for, 14; observation of, 107
PHONOLOGICAL PLAY, 14
PIAGET, J., 12
PLAY: attributes of, 12; cognitive development's link to, 12; environmental print
    in, 13–16; with language, 14–15; language in, 15–16; planning for, 16–19;
    rationale for, 11 13; time required for, 23; vocabulary learned through, 14–16
POLLING ACTIVITY, 57–61
POST OFFICE CENTER, 15*f*
POSTERS, 17
PRESSLEY, M.C., 3
PRETEND PLAY, 13, 15–16
PRINT AWARENESS: and classroom organization, 17; definition of, 2; of
    economically disadvantaged children, 4; observation of, 110
PRIOR, J., 7, 8, 25, 76
PROCESS, 12
PROP BOX, 19, 20*f*, 21*f*
PUZZLES: with and without direct instruction, 8–9; individual activity with, 100;
    overview of, 24; two-piece, 81–83; for use by parents, 119

Q

QUESTIONNAIRE, PARENT, 115*f*
QUESTIONS, 26

R

RANKIN, J., 3
RATCLIFF, N., 17

READINESS, 1

READING FIRST PROGRAM, 4

READING PROFICIENCY: indicators of, 27; predictors of, 6; recent attention to, 1

READING TEXTS. *See* texts

REPRESENTATIONAL PLAY, 13, 15–16

RESEARCH STUDIES, 7, 120–127

RICHGELS, D.J., 6

ROSKOS, K.A., 6, 13, 17, 23

RUST, D., 13

S

SAMPLING, 110, 113

SCHEDULES, 16

SCIENTIST/LABORATORY PROP BOX, 20*f*

SELF-ESTEEM, 13

SHOPPING ACTIVITIES, 119

SHOW AND TELL ACTIVITY, 50

SIGNS, 16–17

SIMMONS, D., 2

SMITH, S., 2, 6

SNYDER, S., 5, 7

SOCIODRAMATIC PLAY, 15–16

SOLITARY PLAY, 12

SOUND PLAY, 14

SOUND RECOGNITION, 2, 110

SPINNER GAME, 95–97

SYNTACTICAL PLAY, 14–15

T

TEACHER-AS-FACILITATOR APPROACH, 4, 8

TEACHERS: comments from, 128–129; expectations of, 2; importance of, 25; modeling of, 25–26; play planning of, 16–19; recommendations for, 118, 129; stories of success from, 117

TEACHING STRATEGIES: best practices in, 3; with environmental print, 19, 22–24. *See also specific strategies*

TEXTS, 5–7

TIME, 23

TIME SAMPLING, 110, 113

TODDLERS, 4

TRAVEL ACTIVITIES, 119

TRAWICK-SMITH, J., 16

TWO-LETTER FOLDER ACTIVITY, 98
TWO-PIECE PUZZLE GAME, 81–83

U–V

U.S. DEPARTMENT OF EDUCATION, 1, 3
VACATION PROP BOX, 20*f*
VENN DIAGRAM, 47
VETERINARIAN PROP BOX, 20*f*
VOCABULARY: learned through play, 14–16; teachers' support for, 2; of toddlers, 4
VUKELICH, C., 7
VYGOTSKY, L.S., 13

W

WALKING ACTIVITIES, 119
WALLS, 16–17, 51–54
WHOLE-TEXT LITERATURE, 3
WOODWARD, V., 6, 7
WORD WALLS, 55
WRITING, 1, 2–3
WRITING CENTER, 15*f*, 17

Y–Z

YAWKEY, T.D., 20
YLISTO, I., 7
YOKOI, Y., 3
ZONE OF PROXIMAL DEVELOPMENT, 13